What Would The Founding Fathers Tell Us Today?

Political Dialogues Between 1789 - 2040

Werner Neff

Copyright 2022

All rights reserved. No part of this text may be reproduced, transmitted, or distributed in any form or by any means without permission in writing from the publisher, except in the case of brief quotations embodied in critical articles or reviews.

Legal & Disclaimer

The content and information in this book is consistent and truthful, and it has been provided for informational, educational, and business purposes only. The texts are fictional discussions. The author cannot be held liable for any omissions and/or errors.

Impressum

ISBN-13 for the printed book: **979-8-88722-911-9**
ISBN-10 for the printed book:
e-book (Kindle) ISBN: 979-8-88722-910-2
Copyright © 2022 Werner Neff
IngramSpark
www.wernerneff.com

Cover Photo:
Writing the Declaration of Independence, 1776
Oil painting by Jean Leon Gerome Ferris, circa 1921
Benjamin Franklin and John Adams sitting, Thomas Jefferson, standing, in Jefferson's office on the corner of Seventh and High (Market) Streets in Philadelphia.

Table of Contents

Introduction 7
1789 9
    The Founding Fathers 9
        Key Points 18
    The Articles of Confederation 19
        Key Points 21
    The Constitutional Convention—A Discussion of
        the Founding Fathers 22
        Key Points 30
    The Declaration of Independence 31
        Key Points 34
    The American Constitution 35
    The Bill of Rights 36
2020 49
    Coming to Washington, D.C., in 2020 49
    The Evening of November 3, 2020 56
    The Political Structure of America 63
    "Why only two parties?" 71
    The Impact of the American 77
    Constitution on Politics 77
        The Role of America's Constitution 83
        in Political Parties 83
    Voting Rights 89
        America's Voting Process 90
        Justifiable? 96
        The Struggle Is Real 101
        Conclusion 111
    Observations 113
    January 7, 2021 122

- Partisan Politics 124
- The Ethics of Democracy 131
  - Conclusion 136
- What Are Democratic Rules? 137
- 2040 139
  - A Look Back 139
- Epilogue 149
- Bibliography 151

Introduction

The Founding Fathers are visiting the United States after two hundred-plus years. What?! What is the purpose? What is the intention of seeing today's political manifestations through the eyes of the Founding Fathers?

The intention of the Founding Fathers was to introduce a new form of government. Tensions with the parliament in London became so great that the colonies gradually separated from Great Britain with the wish to have their own state. It was a long and sometimes painful process.

The result was the passage of the Constitution, which was approved by the constituent states in 1789 and formed the basis of the new nation. With the inauguration of George Washington as the first president, the work of Congress, and the beginning of the tasks of the Supreme Court, all working in a small area in Philadelphia, the experiment began.

What was created between 1760 and 1789 was based on theory. The forms of government in ancient Greece and ancient Rome were the signposts of the new structure. John Locke and Baron de Montesquieu contributed important ideas to the reformation of the state. Thoughts and emotions and fears were expressed in ill-lit rooms where the Founding Fathers pondered, repeatedly, what would best serve the new American nation. This part of America's political history—the unrecorded conversations—we, the people, do not know. We can only surmise.

The new United States was built as a republic, the opposite of a monarchy with hereditary exponents. A republic needs its own rules to meet expectations and demands. These rules are called democratic and are expressed in the noun *democracy*.

Since then, more than two hundred years of history have passed, and actions, events, ideologies, and technologies have shaped the United States of America. Small changes on texts happened over the years, a different understanding of political definitions became common, and a large portion of self-interest on the part of politicians and parties, opinion makers and associations influence the picture of politics today. It is the intention of this book to compare the rules of democracy with contemporary American political life.

To bring this political history to the fore, much research has been done to recreate conversations among the Founding Fathers, both in the 1770s and in recent years, when time travel transports them to Washington DC. We felt that providing the American people with thoughtful conversations by the men who laid the bedrock of our democracy would bring fresh, needed perspective to today's politics.

Americans should feel secure to assume that its governments and institutions function as a system, and that those running the system can be trusted enough to do the right things. After all, America was one of the most democratic nations in the world from the moment of its birth.

With the Constitution in place since 1789, American citizens have the right, and the power, to raise their voices and influence the course of politics. Isn't that a good starting point? Let's get inspired by the Founding Fathers' conversations in this political novel.

1789

The Founding Fathers

A birth happened in 1776 that would significantly impact all the world around it forever after. It began with a "Declaration of Independence," and it was named by the people who gave it life: the people of the United States of America. It was the first country that was not derived from God, nor noble rules. Rather, its birth was orchestrated by a determined group of people who made it their goal to ensure the infant country would stand firm and enforce freedom, justice, and fairness for all its people. It was built to last.

Freedom for all and fairness for all might have seemed like more of a novel idea than a realistic one, but with the determination of this group of people, there would be built-in assurances that the Declaration and Constitution would always be guiding documents. They would be reviewed from time to time and, especially, when they had the need for guidance. This need would ensure America's sustenance, its survival, its very existence.

However, before what we know today as "The United States of America," the Founding Fathers—as they would come to be known—also had an infant country under British colonialist rule. Colonialism was designed to benefit only the colonizer, and to sabotage the colonized. Throughout history, countries that have gained their freedom from colonizers have used the word "Independence", because the amount of subjugation from the colonizer is so great that crucial and considerable efforts have to be made to get freedom as quickly as possible. This was where the role of the "Founding Fathers" came in.

∼∼∼

For two hundred years, the term Founding Fathers has pervaded the history of America, for no telling of the story can be complete without them. Their importance cannot be overemphasized, because the Founders' efforts to liberate America from the colonial British Crown, and to create a new kind of government. Accordingly, this, the first part of our story, attempts to expound on the *mysterious* identities of these Founding Fathers.

In 1774, discontent of British rule was growing quickly among the Colonials. The Founding Fathers were the representatives chosen to voice this discontent on behalf of a majority.

After agreeing to put an end to the grasp of British colonial rule, they decided to take a new stance: they held the first-ever Continental Congress, in Philadelphia, Pennsylvania, on September 5, 1774. Peyton Randolph was president of the Congress, which was a coming together of various delegates from twelve of the thirteen British colonies. At the Congress, the following conversation ensued, informally, at Carpenter Hall.

∼∼∼

John Adams glanced around the table before speaking, calmly but emphatically, "If a reiteration is what will make you understand the emphasis of our statements, then so be it. We have decided that we will not reconcile British authority with colonial freedom."

"But do you understand," George Galloway, a follower of the king of England, responded, "the import of what you are suggesting? Gentlemen, I understand your need to ask for the freedom of your country...."

"Ask?" shouted George Washington, interrupting his companion. "We are not asking our freedom from you. We are *stating* it because you do not have the right to grant us freedom. Our freedom is not subjected to your decision. Our freedom comes from a much higher governor than yours."

John Jay raised his hand to enforce decorum and then spoke, "Before we start playing a game of synonyms, I think what he is trying to say is that you should consult rationality in your approach."

The room grew tense as Patrick Henry cleared his throat to get their attention. "I don't think there is anything more rational than autonomy. If you ask us to consult rationality, you should take that advice yourself."

With that, Jay's face got red with frustration. Joseph Galloway tried to calm him: "You want the truth? America is not ready! A step toward ensuring your absolute autonomy from Britain may lead to division among your States so much that we will have to come to your aid again."

"Well, I hear probabilities," Washington said, with a firm composure.

"See, that is what you just don't get," Galloway started. "We are only trying to be reasonable here. The truth is that you will get your freedom but dissociating it completely from British rule is like removing your anchor from a ship and letting it go off a cliff. You might not be ready for the consequences." He looked at the other men for support, and Dickinson spoke:

"We understand your stance, and we want America's autonomy to be a finite and specified matter, as much as possible, but we want you to know that you have to give us a few more years to work toward America's absolute authority." The room was silent for a few seconds, then Henry stood up and, seeing that he had the floor, took his moment to adjust his coat.

"Gentlemen, we have weighed the cons and pros, and we very much appreciate your advice. But we think there might be some subjectivity in your proposed consequences of our autonomy. We very much agree with you on these probabilities, but we are not unintelligent men. We have put measures in place to combat these ugly probabilities." After this statement, Dickinson and Galloway stood up simultaneously.

"Mr. Washington, if we may reason with you...."

"See, that's what *you* don't understand." Washington would not be silenced. "We have made a collective stance. And while it may seem to you that I am the leader of what you may be terming 'an unreasonable rebellion,' I am not. There is no leader. This decision is borne out of the fact that we have united to make a declaration for personal rights, assembly, liberty, life, and trial by jury, based on our own rules, by our own people, and for our own people...."

"Mr. Washington...," Dickinson interrupted.

"...which also means that we are rejecting the presence of your armies in our nation. You have put them there without our consent, as well as taxation without representation,"

Washington continued, as though he hadn't heard the king's men.

Dickinson tightened his lips. Then, finally, it was clear he had had enough. "You call it your nation; we say they are our colonials."

"Well then, you fail to understand the message," Henry told them point blank. "This is not a negotiation. *This* is a declaration." Dickinson, Galloway, and Jay exchanged worrying meaningful expressions and whispered among themselves.

Jay paused at the door as the king's men started to leave. "If you are worried about how the regulation of America's commerce will be made, we came to a conclusion on that. But, as you pointed out, we are not ideal men alone; we are very realistic. The Parliament can regulate the commerce for a period."

Dickinson moved his head irritatingly. "These terms are ridiculous, and let it be known here and now that the Crown does not agree with these terms or any other terms you might come up with any time soon. We determine when to let our colonies go."

Jay stared at him angrily but calmly. "And when is that?"

"When we say so," Dickinson stated emphatically.

~ ~ ~

Well, as the king's colonial leaders articulated it, freedom without Britain's association was "when we say so," but, this group of people was not about to give up. That same year, the Crown was petitioned about numerous requests and complaints and had done nothing about them since the

1760s. When it was apparent no reply was forthcoming, the Founding Fathers embarked on a strategy to force the Crown's decision. They added a boycott of British goods in America and prohibited the exportation of major goods out of America to England.

This decision was made to force the king's hand to meet their demands. After this, the advocates of the new country, those who today are known as the Founding Fathers, came up with another strategy to get the king to agree to their demands. In 1775, they called for a second Continental Congress.

By the time of the Second Continental Congress, Thomas Jefferson, John Hancock, and Benjamin Franklin had already joined the numbers of Founding Fathers who attended the First Continental Congress. The plan was that all attend the Second Congress, which would be held on May 10, 1775, again in Philadelphia, where the following conversation ensued.

~ ~ ~

"We see you have made some efforts to make good on your demands, and we hope you have made your mind ready for some adjustments in them," John Dickinson started with a cooperative tone.

"I think we have made our stance clear," responded George Washington. "But unfortunately, time has not changed our decision. Especially seeing the reaction of the people against your troops at Lexington and Concord."

"The reactions of the people? Or *your* reactions? You want to tell me you had nothing to do with those hostilities?" John Jay blurted out.

"Gentlemen, remember you are gentlemen. We are not here to trade words or play a game of who is right or wrong. We are here to discuss the future of a nation, and we cannot do this successfully without setting aside our differences," Thomas Jefferson played the role of a peacemaker.

"Well, you set a date for this Congress. We hope that our assumptions are not unfounded—that you've made modifications in some of your demands," Dickinson barked at the Founding Fathers with an obvious air of superiority.

Patrick Henry glanced around the room and settled his gaze on the Colonial leaders. "We hope the decisions are mutual. These modifications are not modifications in their entirety. They are more of accepting the situation of things. Freedom and Independence remain our stance."

"While we get Independence, we know it is not entirely possible to dissociate the Crown from our authority. So, we may agree to the intervention, but this agreement does not make America a puppet under the king through puppet-act decisions from the Crown," Washington declared.

Dickinson and Galloway exchanged looks briefly. "Well, you are finally saying some things that may bring us to the same side of the fence, nevertheless. While the issue of Independence has been resolved, we still feel that you are desperately fighting for your rights rather than the survival of the thirteen American Colonies."

"Our rights are our survival," Jay stated, emphatically.

Dickinson glanced at him surreptitiously and uttered, "As we indicated, Independence is guaranteed, but we will be serving as the provisional government to the governance of the thirteen Colony States. We will see to the establishment of the Navy, and we will not withdraw the New England Army that has converged upon Boston."

The advocates of the new country whispered among themselves until John Adams finally opened with, "As long as the commander-in-chief of the army is an American."

Dickinson and Galloway stood up and spoke the last words, "These changes are not impossible, gentlemen. But as you have pointed out, let us allow a little bit of realism here to make this Congress a fruitful one."

∼ ∼ ∼

Although the conversation above may seem like a sort of inconvenient compromise by the advocates, it was necessary to ensure the absolute Independence of America. The Founding Fathers came to realize this might not be feasible as early as they wanted it. That left them with gradual Independence, which was more realistic in ensuring America's absolute sovereignty from the Crown, and they were not wrong. In fact, they were not wrong at all.

Gradually, America started involving Britain in fewer of its activities and decisions. Though this did not sit well with England, the British started to accept this cut-off as time went by. On June 15, 1775, George Washington was appointed commander-in-chief of the American Army. By 1776, the thirteen American colonies declared themselves "Free and Independent States." Thomas Jefferson drafted his Declaration of Independence, and Benjamin Franklin completed the draft. John Hancock was the first person to sign this Declaration as president of the Second Continental Congress.

Who were the advocates of the new nation? Who became the Founding Fathers of the United States of America later? That is difficult to define. The truth is that over fifty delegates attended the First Continental Congress of 1774. It is a fact that the first Congress saw the absence of Thomas Jefferson, John Hancock, and Benjamin Franklin. These men, among the most well-known Founding Fathers, only attended the Second Continental Congress.

The truth is, there is no need to try to shortlist those among the Founding Fathers, nor to judge who are and are not supposed to be on that list. If fifty people attended the First Continental Congress, they must all be referred to as Founding Fathers. Accordingly, we shall try to make a list of Founding Fathers who did individually outstanding things to further the freedom, independence, growth, and consequent development of America from the time it was just a colony of thirteen states.

These men were advocates who worked hard and consistently to achieve the goals of the new nation, based on Republicanism with democratic rules. These are:

- Benjamin Franklin (1706-1790)
- George Washington (1732-1799)
- John Adams (1735-1826)
- Thomas Jefferson (1743-1826)
- Alexander Hamilton (1744-1804)
- John Jay (1745-1829)
- James Madison (1751-1836)

The truth is that the Founding Fathers did push the absolute Independence of America, but while it may seem that their work was done with that, it had just begun. America had to thrive in order to put to rest the assumptions of its former colonizers, who waited patiently to see its failure.

Thus, we had the birth of the first constitution of America: the Articles of Confederation.

Key Points

- The first Congress was crucial to establishing the Independence of America, as it would enable the Founding Fathers to push for the interests of the country.
- The second Congress was not an outright compromise on the part of the Founding Fathers, but a realization that demand for complete autonomy was not a realistic approach to America's Independence yet.
- The term "Founding Fathers" does not refer only to a group of men but must include all the people who contributed immensely to securing America's Independence.

The Articles of Confederation

The Articles of Confederation of November 1777 were, for all intents and purposes, the first Constitution of the United States of America. We cannot imagine the kind of strategy and delicacy the Founding Fathers had to employ to bring the "Articles" for developing the thirteen colonies. It had to be as perfect and enforceable as possible if America was going to thrive as a nation.

It fell to the Second Continental Congress to draft the first constitution of America: The Articles of Confederation. By then, they had already seen enough of what a central authority like the British government could do, so they tried to avert what they thought would be the mistakes and pitfalls accordingly.

You might think the word "Strategy" is being overused in association with the Founding Fathers, but, truly, you must believe it can never be overemphasized. The Articles of Confederation were designed in such a way that there would be a convenient, deliberate, and subtle exclusion of Britain's involvement in America's affairs. Furthermore, the document had to rule out any and all efforts of neo-colonialism in any form. Therefore, a Confederation of Sovereign States was established, and this Confederation would be responsible for ratifying The Articles of Confederation. By March 1, 1781, the thirteen colony states did indeed ratify America's first constitution.

In the end, much power was vested in the thirteen original colony states that made up the Confederation—while very little power was given to the central government. As we shall see, this was done deliberately, to avoid dictatorial tendencies that could wreck young America.

The first constitution made good on some of its intentions—like strengthening the individual states that made up the federation. But it also made way for self-governance in colony states—which was, in fact, the goal of the Founding Fathers. This measure would secure the autonomy of America because it would truly be known and felt by all Americans, as well as by the states that made up the nation.

This separation of powers made it possible for power to be vested in the Confederation States and Congress, which was heretofore referred to as "The Congress." It had the power to appoint military officers, determine the value of American money, issue bills of credit, borrow money, and regulate foreign affairs. These powers all seem to have been spelled out; yet there were several things that rendered the first constitution impractical for the growth of America.

True, the Articles of Confederation enabled The Congress to enact the U.S. Northwest Ordinances (1784-1787), which were to ensure a procedure based on equitable land settlement in Midwest America. However, the constitution had many faults, which would have to be discussed and critically analyzed by the Founding Fathers if the Articles were to serve the nation.

This discussion is what led to the Constitutional Convention of 1789.

Key Points

- The Articles of Confederation were a creation of the Second Continental Congress.
- Although Britain's constitution was supposed to be the model, the Articles of Confederation were fashioned to be a complete departure from Britain's constitution, because they rendered the central government too powerful. This was inimical to the development of the new nation.

The Constitutional Convention—A Discussion of the Founding Fathers

After eight years of putting the first constitution of America to use and seeing that it didn't produce all it was intended to, the Founding Fathers—Thomas Jefferson, John Adams, Benjamin Franklin, Alexander Hamilton, John Jay, James Madison, and George Washington—met several times to discuss how the document could best be restructured. As you read these discussions, you have to understand they are the highlight of history itself.

Picture a fireplace with five agile men seated in the room; two young women—secretaries—are seated at the far side of the room. The mood is light-hearted, but still serious with anticipation of the task ahead of them. There is not very much light in the room, and the cushions are arranged in a square structure in the middle.

~~~

Alexander Hamilton is resting his leg on the extended part of a chair, and he is speaking as we listen in: "I'm just glad we made that decision. I mean...it marked a different height in the development of America."

"Okay...slow your roll, and go easy on that cigar, 'cause it looks like you are about to choke," John Adams warned.

Hamilton did indeed choke, and the others laughed. Then he joined in the laugh, too, while still choking.

"You are right...very right. I mean, we didn't even expect that much success on the Articles of Confederation. But, still, it's helped our country for the past seven...eight years?" John Jay pointed out.

"Eight years," James Madison replied. "The Brits are probably sucking it in where they are."

They all laughed again. Benjamin Franklin entered the room, aided by his security men.

"And why are you laughing when we are on the brink of trouble, young men?" Franklin asked mockingly.

"Good old Benjamin! We thought you wouldn't join us so early," Hamilton said, standing up to shake hands with him.

"Oh...keep the sarcasm, Alexander. If you were my age, you'd be telling all Americans to treat you like an egg or America would collapse," Franklin barked at the younger man and sat down.

"Or wipe his butt!" Adams cackled at his own humor.

As the men laughed, George Washington came into the room with Thomas Jefferson and his first words were, "Are we wiping butts here? Or talking sense?"

"My General," Jay shouted, standing up. He passed some cigarettes to the men. Jefferson refused them.

"Thanks, Jay, but not now," Jefferson pushed way his hand away gently and sat down. "I have an address to give tomorrow, and I fear I might catch cold this night."

"How's your wife, Jay?" Washington asked.

"She's fine. She sends her greetings, too," Jay told Washington, rubbing his hands together.

"Well," Jefferson began. "The night is still young, and we must make the most of the time we have. We are going to be here for a while, gentlemen, and…although what we discuss here is not final in its entirety, it will be crucial for the amendment of the current constitution of America. We are making history here, and I hope every one of us is here with his observations on the Articles of Confederation and how we changed it in the Constitutional Convention."

"Well…I think since we have underlined the problems with the Articles of Confederation, we can just simply move on to the sections we changed," Adams replied.

Franklin laughed shortly. "Underlined? The last time we met, you almost threw a cup of coffee at Thomas for saying the Articles were a test-run project. Ain't that right, Jamie?"

Madison laughed. "It was indeed a funny one."

"So, why exactly are we gathered, young men?" Jefferson asked jokingly.

"The reason is not far-fetched. About a year ago, these seven strong headed but mostly bald men…."

They all laughed as Franklin continued "… sat down to draft a constitution for America. Gentlemen, thirteen years later, and here we are. The Articles of Confederation were a success. And the document has served its purpose. In fact, I think we all deserve a round of applause."

The men clapped for themselves, and a young man came in to serve another round of gin.

"I don't think our work was done," Franklin explained. "The most important thing is that we needed to reconsolidate the presence of The Congress, considering its lack of effectiveness in managing affairs that needed urgent attention."

"My exact thoughts!" Adams replied. "I mean, we did have a central government, but it was too weak to make decisions on its own…"

"…and not all the Colony States were present when we needed them to vote," Madison finished Adams's sentence and continued.

"True, their presence was needed, but the fact that The Congress has no power to enforce its request to the colony states was also a huge problem. So, you know what we needed? A strong, cohesive central government that can put these states in check and rule America as effectively as possible."

"And here we have, Mr. President, a man of the people," Hamilton remarked.

Washington laughed heartily.

"I think we all know that. It is no gainsaying that the firm central government rule of Britain did no good in influencing our decision. But the writing on the wall was clear. The Congress was ineffective," Franklin bemoaned.

"Exactly," Washington agreed. "And there was no money to conduct the activities of America successfully. We could print and borrow money, but it was useless because we couldn't return it. The colony states paid little in taxes, while some did not even pay at all. Gentlemen, I mean, as Jay brought up, 1786 was a mess. We could not pay our outstanding debts to other countries."

"Did you remember that we also could not pay our 625-men army troops? Did you hear that some soldiers in Ohio threatened to desert, while others considered mutiny?" Hamilton asked.

"Well, well," Franklin started. "You can't blame them. The fact that they waited that long was out of patriotism. If we want our citizens to be patriotic, we need to show them why. Patriotism is borne out of willingness and love for one's country, and we are bringing that love back."

Adams sipped some gin and cleared his throat. "Not to mention that the 1783 Treaty of Paris we signed with the Brits had no effect on the colony states. Some of them even violated that treaty!"

"Well, John, when it comes to state legislatures waging war, you sure do know that the central government was a figurehead," Hamilton said.

Washington glanced around briefly and spoke loudly, "I think it's time I say what is on all our minds. We switched to the presidential form of governance. There was a need for a president, a vice president, and the cabinet members of the president to ensure proper executive administration."

"Hear, hear. Based on that, they have the power...in fact, absolute power to organize their own elections without interference from the central government," Jay chimed in, sounding, suddenly, a little groggy with gin.

"And we ensured absolute separation of powers from the executive, legislative, and judicial arms. These organs of government can only function well if they are properly separated."

At that, Washington clapped his hands enthusiastically. "See, Ben gets it...so we don't have the problem of a too-strong central government."

"Hmm...unicameral legislature is equivalent to more problems for the legislature," Madison pointed out. "Especially in the case of proper separation of powers. I think we all know that separation of powers should be established and enforced in each level of government."

"Well said. So, a bicameral legislature for each state of the confederation," Jay ordered.

"States of the confederation? There ain't no confederation anymore, man! John, you are sleeping already?" Washington asked, jokingly, as everyone laughed.

"Someone, get a hold of this man!" Jefferson joined in, still laughing.

Jay adjusted in his chair to restore his dignity. "So, by bicameral, we mean a House of Representatives and a Senate."

"Exactly!" Hamilton affirmed, then paused. "Well, I don't think the judicial arm of governance should be that hard to define. I mean, based on the democratic principles America was founded on, the power of the judiciary was automatically vested in federal courts, and they have the power to interpret the laws for any crime based on The Constitution."

"Yeah...yeah...you are right. The U.S. Judicial Act is not a big deal," Washington conceded, slowly nodding his head.

Hamilton laughed, surprised. "That was not what you told me on the golf course."

"Well, I was angry that you were winning that day," Washington grumbled, as he tried to "hide" his face by drinking his gin.

"I did beat you that day," Hamilton laughed, grinning from ear to ear.

"You cheated! You little cheat!" Washington blurted out as the men laughed.

"Oh...suck it up, George," Franklin said. "You know you cheated the last time we played, too."

"When was that? Ten years ago?" Washington asked sarcastically. The men laughed loudly again.

"Now to the Declaration of Independence," Franklin nearly whispered, softly.

"Oh...you all know I had the idea for the preamble of The Constitution...it was supposed to start with..., "We are the united people of America, and we will...."

"Pass!" Jay interrupted Franklin and turned to join the laughter that had already started.

"He sounded like he was reading poetry!" Hamilton remarked, as the men did indeed start another round of laughter.

"Good ol' Ben," Washington pronounced, shaking his head. "Maybe you should take up poetry when your work with America is done...."

"...which is never!" Adams grumbled.

At that, the laughter rose to another heightened pitch. This time, the secretaries in the room joined in too, while the young man came in to serve still more gin.

"Funny. But let's talk about the Declaration of Independence," Jefferson half-asked his colleagues, suddenly becoming very serious.

~ ~ ~

The above discussion is, foremost, about the review of The Articles of Confederation. This part has to do with the separation of powers among the three primary organs of government that were created by the Founding Fathers that night and others. Keep in mind that thirteen states ratified the first Constitution on March 1, 1781.

However, that first version of the Constitution strengthened the thirteen states of the confederation to such a degree that the central government—which we know as the federal government today—was more of a figurehead that couldn't do anything unless the presence of the states was guaranteed. The worst thing was that, before decisions could be made, at least eleven of the thirteen states had to come around. But getting eleven of the thirteen states to attend The Congress was a novel idea. Only nine states usually showed up for The Congress, which left many items untouched.

The Congress was in enormous debt at the end of 1786, and the United States government had too much unsettled debt to other governments. The states did not pay their taxes and were so strong that they could not be checked by the central government. They violated the Articles of the Treaty of Paris (1783) by raising armies, prosecuting wartime activities, and even waging war themselves.

The first attempt of the Constitutional Convention, therefore, was to overhaul the whole confederation by setting up a new form of government: a presidential form of government, where the president would be the head of the executive branch as well as head of state and government. He would also have a vice president. The legislature would be bicameral; that is, it would have a Senate and a House of Representatives whose legislators would represent each state of the union, to ensure autonomy and proper separation of powers. The Judicial Act would be enforced to establish solidly the power of the judiciary in federal courts.

Once this problem of governance was tackled, the Founding Fathers knew America was on track for a more effective and autonomous government, one that could bring the states back in check and make sure the country would not be relying on run-away debt. After that, they could move on to tackle other problems.

Key Points

- During their conversation, the Founding Fathers discovered that they were wrong not to make the central government powerful, because The Articles of Confederation empowered the colony states at the expense of the central government.
- They also discussed how they were able to overhaul the system to create a new form of government that would be suitable for the complete autonomy of America.

The Declaration of Independence

Alexander Hamilton was speaking, "...but I still think it should have started with...," when all the men drowned him out with choruses of "noooo."

"You all know we did a hard job with the Brits, right?" Benjamin Franklin reminded them.

"I can never forget the look on old James' face!" John Adams said, laughing.

"Well. You know what they say, 'The oppressed do not get their freedom by begging the morality of their oppressor,'" Franklin said.

"I'm sorry...but was there morality to beg?" John Jay asked as they all laughed.

"Jay!" James Madison exclaimed. They all exchanged looks before breaking out in roaring laughter again.

"Funny that we thought the First Continental Congress was almost a waste of time. It did lead to the buildup of our success at the Second Continental Congress," Adams pointed out.

George Washington stood up to stretch himself. "I can't believe we took our American pride to that room and marched up to their noses, saying, 'We are free from you!'"

"Gentlemen, I believe we shall be remembered for eternity for the Declaration of Independence. We made America free from colonialist rule...," Madison declared.

"And neo-colonialist rule," Adams added. "We had a problem getting all thirteen states to attend The Congress, and Britain thought they could actually get them all the way from that part of the world?"

The men laughed.

Franklin yawned. "Yet, our efforts on July 4, 1776, were mostly propagated through *The Federalist*, written by our most notable and viable men here: Alexander, James, and Jay. I cannot believe you all wrote eighty-five articles and essays to support the Constitution. Whose idea was that? Alexander, I know it was you!"

Hamilton raised his eyebrows. "Well...it was a... collective effort."

They laughed again.

"But if you all had not written something about the purpose of the Constitution and why it had to be revised... There were so many things flying around that did no justice to the amount of selflessness we put into that Constitution," Jefferson said.

"True...1787 was a rough year. All those late nights we spent in my office comparing notes and making sure we didn't leave any stone unturned. How Madison was so intent about advocating a commercial republic rather than 'Rule by Majority,'" Hamilton pointed out, quoting with his fingers waving.

"You know," Madison started, "it got to the point that I swore I was overthinking it. And do you know how we almost didn't support you when you brought up that Bill of Rights thing?"

"My best part," Franklin recollected, "is where he emphasized that there is actually no need to add a Bill of Rights separately to the Constitution, since we have various provisions of the Constitution that already talk about that. The logic behind that is just amazing. I am proud of you, Alexander," Franklin smiled looking at the younger man. Hamilton nodded shyly.

"Hear, hear," Jay declared.

Jefferson glanced at the men. "And we all know that what people enunciate as 'checks and balances' today was laid out by Madison's extensive analogy on it among the organs of government. I love that it made the Constitution as democratic and transparent as we intended it to be."

"We the people," Madison proclaimed.

"That is the Preamble of the Constitution, James. We are talking about *The Federalist*," Hamilton corrected his colleague.

"Let the old man awake from his slumber peacefully," Jefferson remarked, and the men laughed with good cheer.

~ ~ ~

The Federalist, now called *The Federalist Papers*, was a list of 85 articles and essays written by Alexander Hamilton, John Jay, and James Madison to propagate the 1789 Constitution and explain its provisions more extensively to the people directly. *The Papers* clearly explained federalism and checks and balances in the U.S. system, the Bill of Rights, and the Judicial Act in careful detail.

The first seventy-seven of *The Papers* were published in the *Independent Journal*, *The Daily Advertiser*, and *The New York Packet*, around April to October of 1787. Consequently, the remaining eight *Papers* were published between June 14 and August 16, 1788.

It should be noted that the major reason for writing *The Federalist Papers* was to influence voters to ratify the Constitution. By carefully describing every part of the Constitution so that the general public could see and understand what exactly they were being asked to vote for, *The Papers* also ensured the support of the citizens, thereby securing America's growth and consequent development.

It is, therefore, not surprising that, in the very first *Paper* in *The Federalist*, the writers clearly stated:
"It has been frequently remarked that it seems to have been reserved to the people of this country, by their conduct and example, to decide the important question, whether societies of men are really capable or not, of establishing good government from reflection and choice, or whether they are forever destined to depend, for their political constitutions, on accident and force."

Key Points

- This part discusses how the Founding Fathers orchestrated the Declaration of Independence, which led to the complete Independence of America from colonialist and neo-colonialist grasp.
- *The Federalist Papers* were written by Alexander Hamilton, James Madison, and John Jay to ensure that the people would see the essence of the 1789 Constitution and clear up whatever assumptions and issues they may have had with the governing document.

The American Constitution

The writing of the American Constitution in 1789 is a major coup in human history. Its importance is undisputed; indeed, the Constitution, together with the Bill of Rights, has served as a model for other countries as well.

Even so, the good functioning and its wide acceptance does not only depend on the text; it also depends on its unwritten parts. The unspoken (and today, well understandable) truth is that a written constitution is never enough to guide a country's decisions—even though that is all it is meant to be. It is not a question of whether or not America made some deliberate efforts to circumvent democratic processes.

The Founding Fathers created a constitution for America based on the state of America in their time. During that period, America was far from being a world power. In fact, it was still struggling under Britain's neo-colonialist tendencies.

Put simply, democratic norms have unwritten rules of the game, a kind of fundamental code of conduct. They must be widely accepted, respected, and even enforced by all members of that community.

The Bill of Rights

After the Preamble, the Bill of Rights opens the Constitution document. On October 2, 1789, President George Washington sent copies of the twelve amendments that comprise "The Bill" to The Congress, which adopted them. Over time, ten of the twelve were also adopted and ratified by three-fourths of the States. These ten amendments, known as the Bill of Rights, have been referred to as the "most crucial" part of the Constitution.

Historically, the Bill of Rights has its roots in the Magna Carta of 1215 and the English Bill of Rights of 1689 (the Glorious Revolution), which was a call against the colonial struggle by the king and Parliament. The Virginia Declaration of Rights of 1776, as well as the Northwest Ordinance of 1787, were earlier documents.

Few people really pay attention to why these ten amendments are called the Bill of Rights, and whether they are enforceable and as fair as they seem.

So, before we begin, below are each of the first ten Rights that make up "The Bill." This will aid you in understanding the conversation that will ensue afterward.

First Amendment

Congress shall make no law respecting an establishment of religion or prohibiting the free exercise thereof; or abridging the freedom of speech, or of the press, or the right of the people peaceably to assemble, and petition the government for a redress of grievances.

Second Amendment

A well-regulated militia, being necessary to the security of a free state, the right of the people to keep and bear arms, shall not be infringed.

Third Amendment

No soldier shall, in time of peace be quartered in any house, without the consent of the Owner, nor in time of war, but in a manner to be prescribed by law.

Fourth Amendment

The right of the people to be secure in their persons, houses, papers, and effects, against unreasonable searches and seizures, shall not be violated, and no warrants shall issue, but upon probable cause, supported by oath or affirmation, and particularly describing the place to be searched, and the persons or things to be seized.

Fifth Amendment

No person shall be held to answer for a capital, or otherwise infamous crime, unless on a presentment or indictment of a grand jury, except in cases arising in the land or naval forces, or in the militia, when in actual service in time of war or public danger; nor shall any person be subject for the same offense to be twice put in jeopardy of life or limb; nor shall be compelled in any criminal case to be a witness against himself, nor be deprived of life, liberty, or property, without due process of law; nor shall private property be taken for public use, without just compensation.

Sixth Amendment

In all criminal prosecutions, the accused shall enjoy the right to a speedy and public trial, by an impartial jury of the state and district wherein the crime shall have been committed, which district shall have been previously ascertained by law, and to be informed of the nature and cause of the accusation; to be confronted with the witnesses against him; to have compulsory process for obtaining witnesses in his favor, and to have the assistance of counsel for his defense.

Seventh Amendment

In suits at common law, where the value in controversy shall exceed twenty dollars, the right of trial by jury shall be preserved, and no fact tried by a jury, shall be otherwise reexamined in any court of the United States, then according to the rules of the common law.

Eighth Amendment

Excessive bail shall not be required, nor excessive fines imposed, nor cruel and unusual punishments inflicted.

> ## Ninth Amendment
>
> The enumeration in the Constitution, of certain rights, shall not be construed to deny or disparage others retained by the people.
>
> ## Tenth Amendment
>
> The powers not delegated to the United States by the Constitution, nor prohibited by it to the States, are reserved to the States respectively, or to the people.

~~~

"Mr. President, I hope the first amendment of the Bill of Rights protects me on my right to speech, because your outfit at the Inauguration was a sight indeed!" John Jay declared laughing.

George Washington scoffed. "No need for euphemism. I invoke my right to protest the authenticity of that outfit."

They all laughed.

"I...I thought I looked splendid as I stood on the balcony of Federal Hall and took my oath," the President pronounced.

Benjamin Franklin unbuttoned his coat and said: "It was a legendary moment."

"Indeed, it was," James Madison agreed. "But that outfit was not legendary!"

The men started laughing again, and this time Washington joined in.

"I think the First Amendment really provides people the rights to speech, religion, and protest, as we hoped it would. I mean, George, did you see what a newspaper wrote about your first thirty days in office?" John Adams asked.

"It was too opinionated," Thomas Jefferson corrected Adams.

"But isn't that how we expected it to be?" Alexander Hamilton asked.

"Yes," Franklin agreed, "...but do you remember when we had to enforce how American soldiers cannot force homeowners out of their homes? I think that is a credit to us, considering that we didn't fashion it after the British Law—they permitted their soldiers to take over private homes during the Revolutionary War."

President Washington waved his finger in the air. "Although some people in The Congress did kick against the Third Amendment. But the question I raised is: To what extent do we have to be such a huge inconvenience to citizens when we are defending national security?"

"See?" Adams asked. "Mr. President, that was exactly the problem that bald man in The Congress had with the Third Amendment. I mean, if we are protecting citizens as they have charged us to, then why shouldn't they be willing to give up a few things to support the government and their country?"

"John, they pay taxes," Hamilton reminded his colleague emphatically.

"I know, Alexander," Adams replied. "But that bald man ...what was his name?

"O'Connor," Madison filled in the blank.

"John O'Connor added a logical stance to it," Adams stated. "Yet, if we look at it closely, security does come with some inconvenience."

Franklin shook his head in disagreement. "Well, let's look at it radically. How do you feel when a group of soldiers walk into your home in the middle of the night and tell you to take your properties out into the cold night, because the laws permit them to take your home temporarily, while they are…protecting national security? Come on, John."

"I don't think it's as simple as that," Adams asserted conclusively.

"It's not the Third Amendment that causes so much uproar as the publications and protests people are making about the Fourth Amendment," Jefferson was adamant. "People are claiming it looks good on paper, but it is only based on theory."

"In their defense," Hamilton offered, "I think there have been a few cases where there have been unreasonable search and seizures of individual properties."

"But didn't most of those cases actually result in the confirmation of the speculations that provoked the action?" Jay asked, categorically.

"Come on, John. That still does not justify the action," Madison demanded.

"But the result is justified?" Jay asked.

Washington piped up to respond. "As president, I think it's only reasonable when I say that the populace does not understand what we're going through in trying to make America safe. We might have some level of stability, but we are still a young country. Attempts have been made to sabotage our integrity and influence in the international sphere."

"George, you do know you can't accept that you sanction the behavior of the armed forces about the Third Amendment," Franklin reminded the former President.

"I'm just saying they should not be blamed for something they didn't do," Washington said. "For all we know, they may even be adhering to the instructions of the unit heads. When a security problem breaks out in America, people condemn us and ask if all we do is sleep in the Franklin house. When we try to prevent these occurrences, these same people harass them." Washington said, heaving a heavy sigh.

Franklin, on the other hand, was wearing a blank expression. "For me, it's double-sided for the people. They accept the Rights that favor them well and reject the ones that constrain them. Look at the way they easily claimed the Fifth Amendment."

"But aren't rights supposed to favor people?" Madison asked.

"If rights were only to favor people, murderers would walk free," Washington stated categorically.

"I mean...the Fifth Amendment gives people the right against self-incrimination!" Jay shouted to be heard.

"Careful, Jay, or you might incriminate yourself," Washington joked. He had obviously intended to move the conversation along by lightening it up a bit.

They all understood their leader and smiled.

Then Franklin stared around the room and cleared his throat. "Even the Sixth Amendment protects the right of people accused of crimes. The right to an impartial and speedy trial and jury is all about that."

"Gentlemen," Madison interrupted. "It's even easy to get over all of these amendments. But there are some people who still think there are plenty of flaws in them."

"Plenty of flaws? What people?" Washington asked dismissively.

Madison sighed deeply. "George, what were the things we really emphasized when we wanted to draft the Bill of Rights?"

"Jamie, you know we emphasized a lot of things. It's not my fault that only ten out of the twelve amendments got ratified," Washington articulated in a serious tone.

Franklin barked a laugh. "A child plays truant at school—blame it on the president. Snow falls more than it should—blame it on the president. People have grave accidents with horses—it's the president's fault." Then, all the men joined in laughter, except Hamilton.

"Well, Mr. President, pertaining to freedom—what was our emphasis on?" he persisted.

"You tell me, Alexander," Washington responded, sipping his gin gently and looking straight at Hamilton.

"It was on national freedom, political freedom, and individual freedom," Hamilton stated categorically.

"I don't see what or where the problem is," Adams chimed in. "If you examine National Freedom, we've been free from the Crown's control for quite some time now. We are making our own rules. I mean—here we are making reviews of America's second Constitution."

"And for political freedom, the people made their choice by accepting the election of George as their president. How much more does it get than the fact that the American governance has been of the people, by the people, and for the people?" Franklin reminded his colleagues.

Hamilton glanced around at them for a few seconds and then calmly added, "You mean for *some* people."

"Oh my God...Hamilton, suck it up," Washington argued, banging the gin bottle on the table.

"Your wife owns the first private orphanage in New York, and she is also a well-known philanthropist. If you ask me, I'll say women are catching up with men."

"It may be true, but there are some social structures that weren't put there automatically by men," Jay said.

"And what would happen if we actually allowed women to rule? Do they have the know-how of governance as we do? I'm not trying to sound like I think women should be without rights now, but in the same way I wouldn't trust a laborer with the affairs of the governance of America, I wouldn't entirely trust a woman to run America," Washington declared with finality.

"If they have limited knowledge, that does not take away their ability to rule," Jefferson argued, trying to weigh both sides.

"Even if we wanted to, Alexander, and we all agreed to let a woman take over the reins of some of our affairs, what would the American people think? You make it sound like we make this sole decision. We don't. If a woman should run for the presidency...," Franklin started, as some of the men were starting to laugh.

"...and win," Franklin continued over their laughter, "it will be because the American people want her. It's still a democracy, remember?"

"Yes, Alexander, we don't determine these things entirely," Adams chimed in, trying to pacify what threatened to become the revisiting of a now old argument.

"Yes...but what about those of the people we can determine?" Hamilton insisted.

"What people?" Madison asked, confused.

"Dark-skinned people," Hamilton spoke back, calmly, but firmly.

"The slaves?" Adams asked, incredulous.

Washington shifted uncomfortably on the cushion and called for more gin. "Hamilton, we talked about this. Some things take time. There are things we just can't do drastically."

"Well, in George's defense, we did suffer many years under British rule," Franklin pointed out.

Hamilton was having none of it. "But does that mean the people whose independence we fought for should be subjected to slavery?"

"The people are not subjected to slavery. Some people are, and those people who are slaves are slaves because of the circumstance surrounding their being," Adams threw out his words and then sipped some gin.

"Well, I don't think a person's skin color makes him less human. I try not to refer to the subject of slavery, but haven't those people been slaves for some hundred...two hundred years?" Madison asked.

Washington looked away and waved his hand dismissively. "Gentlemen, you sound like we don't want slavery abolished, as if we were benefitting from it ourselves. We are not. Do you think I...I want to rule a country where some people are free and some are bonded?"

"I don't think so," Jefferson said, unsure.

"I am the first president of the United States of America. Everything I do and say is being watched. You want my tenure as the first president to be marred by a decision that will make everyone hate me? Alexander, I love your viewpoint, and I accept it, but the American people are not ready for that kind of change." Washington had spoken with his familiar tone of finality.

Franklin gestured with his hands to show support. "Slavery will be abolished in America, but we can't be the ones to do that…I mean, not yet. It's too sudden, and any drastic decision like that may lead to George's impeachment. It is something that must be worked on gradually."

For a moment, Washington kept his gaze on Alexander Hamilton. Then he stood up, walked over to him, and placed his hands on the younger man's shoulders.

"Remember how we were so mad at the First Continental Congress, and we wanted to get absolute independence without Britain's involvement? Did it work out?"

"No," Hamilton spoke softly.

"But what happened when we decided to get independence and accept their involvement?"

Hamilton did not say anything. Instead, he pursed his lips and glanced at the men in the room.

Washington, with compassion for his younger colleague, ended the conversation with this: "It's not turning a blind eye to the problem; it's *pretending* we are turning a blind eye to the problem. The 1789 Constitution will be amended, maybe many times over, and slavery will eventually be abolished. But it is still the government of the people, by the people, and for the people."

"Hear, hear!" Adams shouted out. "Bring more gin!"

~~~

There seems to be some sort of intensity in the discussion about the 1789 Bill of Rights. The reason for this is not far-fetched. Rights tend to be delicately measured—under-measured or over-measured—depending on an individual's viewpoint with respect to the type of right being discussed.

The major emphasis on the Bill of Rights during its draft was freedom—that was the original goal, and this freedom was to be expressed in three ways:

- National Freedom: America should make its own rules without the inclusion of decisions or influences from foreign forces.
- Political Freedom: The citizens of America should have the right to free elections, to elect the people of their own choice, and to be governed under their own laws; and
- Individual Freedom: As defined, the free choice of living as long as others are not harmed.

True, the Bill of Rights contained the goal of freedom, which was the major goal of the Founding Fathers when "The Bill" was drafted on September 25, 1789. It focused on National Freedom, Political Freedom, and Individual Freedom. Still, the problem of the Bill catering to certain people's rights leaves much to be desired, which was a problem the Founding Fathers hoped to combat.

The journey of the Founding Fathers, in reviewing the 1789 Constitution, started with the First Continental Congress because it was the major stage of America's independence from Britain. Upon gaining their independence—although not absolute—the country embarked on the Articles of Confederation for the thirteen colony states of America. As the Founding Fathers watched the Articles of Confederation in action, they saw serious ineffectiveness between the ways the states and central government struggled; from that, the 1789 Constitution was birthed. Though it shows that the Fathers really committed a lot to the independence and freedom of America, it only signals the continuation, and some may dare say, the beginning of the hard parts of their work for America.

- The Founding Fathers' discussions about the Bill of Rights were to examine their work on the amendments so far. Then they were to step back again, to see if each amendment was serving its purpose.
- The end of their discussion indicated that the Bill of Rights still had many reviews and adjustments to under-go, as it did not cater to the rights of some people.

2020

Coming to Washington, D.C., in 2020

As we have seen, it is possible for history to offer us a glance into a few of the many conversations the Founding Fathers may have enjoyed as they met their challenge of securing the newborn country. History also affords us the legacies of the great men. We know, for instance, that many of them remained active all the rest of their lives, serving as they could to support the political life of the United States. Some served as president, vice president, treasurer, ambassador, and Supreme Court justice. While we know about some of their families, their households, their lives, and loves—and foibles—they remain, still, our celebrated Founding Fathers.

What we do not and cannot know about the Founders of the first country that ever stated its commitments to National Freedom, Political Freedom, and Individual Freedom is what they might have been thinking about those citizens who would come long after them—what would *they* do with the country they would inherit? We can only speculate what their lively conversations might have sounded like if the Founding Fathers were to visit, once again, the site of the first-ever Continental Congress, in Philadelphia, and perhaps the nation's capital, Washington, D.C., in the year 2020.

Perhaps their conversations might sound something like this:

∼ ∼ ∼

George Washington, first to reach the street in Philadelphia after exiting their bus, made much of there being streets that were all paved. "I cannot recognize this city anymore," he admitted, "nor may I, I fear, be able to find my way around."

Thomas Jefferson noted that they did not see many people walking in the streets, "as we did in our days. They seem to move in covered wagons now, but nothing like those we are familiar with."

Washington, fascinated by the pavements, next moved his eyes up to the few houses he saw. "They are so tall, and everything seems so solidly built, as if to last forever. What say you, Alexander?"

Hamilton, still at his general's right arm, attempted to express his own feelings, "The smell in the streets is so different. I do not smell waste—how do they dispose of all that waste with these many people at once? Neither do I smell sweat—rather, only the fragrances of roses and the flowers that abound at every corner shop keep. My God! I pray they have cherished liberty as well as scents for the senses," he told the others, shaking his head with wonder.

Jefferson, peeking into the windows of passing cars, continued to comment on what his eyes could not fathom. "I saw them behind a window, and inside they use a wheel to move left and right—"

"But there is a noise coming out of their wagons," John Adams declared, "and not only that, there's an odious smell also. I've never come across anything like it with the horses. Strange."

"What's really strange about their wagons is that they just stop moving all of a sudden." This came from James Madison, who had been staring in awe at all the new machines that seemed to be everywhere he looked. "Sometimes they stand still for some minutes, as if the fire brigade is running by with their buckets. And there are so many of these wagons that they block everything. It's a wonder any business can be underway in this city. Look at that, John," he called to Adams.

But Jefferson, ever the fashionista, suddenly had eyes only for the ways the people were dressed. "They look so differently dressed compared to 1789! You can hardly distinguish between rich and poor—how *do* they tell the difference in these years? In some cases, it's even difficult to determine women from men!"

John Jay, meanwhile, was falling in love with all the restaurants that lined the sidewalks, each with its own colors and pictures of their fine foods. "Look at these places, gentlemen, glass wherever you look. Amazing—oh, and this: people drinking in the streets...out of what appear to be paper glasses with some kind of top on them so the beverage will not pour out as they walk...."

"And many of them seem to be carrying two small pieces of bread," Jefferson reported, as if he longed to be one such sandwich carrier. "I'd wager there's something between those small pieces. It's very convenient, I'll say. They can carry their food and eat in the streets wherever they go. Obviously, they put a pretty value on eating wherever they are, these days. That must be why they look so well fed."

Through the hustle and bustle of Philadelphia, Washington remained mostly silent after noting that houses seemed no longer to be placed on the main streets of the city. Hamilton, ever doting on the long-retired first president, took his silent stance alongside him.

After a while, Washington began to reminisce. "When we traveled to the new capital city, the one they named after me, we used that big stagecoach—do you remember, Alexander? It was all metal and glass, and it seemed to hold dozens of people at once. What did you make of that?" Washington asked.

"Perhaps they use that stagecoach to encourage the people to meet their neighbors," Hamilton responded. "The seats are big and comfortable—and it certainly is economical. I think it's a good thing to have the people gathering in a variety of ways; the coach must be only one way. What do you think, Thomas?" Hamilton asked.

"We arrived at Union Station, didn't we? Why do you think they named it Union? Is that an allusion to the United States as the new country?" Jay asked. "The new city is something to behold, though. It's worthy of any president, former or yet to become. Remember how we talked about the principles of how the streets and buildings should be placed?"

"The basic idea we had was a triangle as layout," Adams recalled, as he ran ahead to catch up with the others when he heard the men talking about Washington, D.C. "Now they name the streets to the state names and then add the streets on one side with A, B, and C, etc., and then numbers on the other side. Interesting, don't you think?"

"Quite smart, I'd say," Madison agreed.

"And the place of work for the president is also his residence—that's convenient," Washington said. "It's a nice building, but why is it so complicated to knock at the door? There are fences everywhere, and police officers—some of whom are women—that must please you, Alexander. I never thought I would see the day when a mere whisp of a girl would be a police officer to protect the president. Strange."

"...or that the buildings would be so huge, tall, and majestic," Adams added. "Did you see the Supreme Court? And the Capitol, the building on the hill? Amazing...and that beautiful memorial they built for you, Thomas. The people's love for you shows no bounds..."

"Oh, don't carry on like that, John," Jefferson pleaded. "I do agree with you about the buildings in Washington's city, though. All in the classical style, just as we imagined it might look. I am surprised that there is no swampland anymore—how do you think they managed to do that? Channels? Holes?"

"The tour we took into the Capitol building was a surprise," Hamilton acknowledged. "Painted portraits of unknown faces all around. I must admit I was curious about who all those people were. And to go on that tour one had to show a photo ID—what do you think a photo is? Or an ID? When I asked the woman, she looked at me as if I were a stranger from another land. She explained it was a small document with my likeness and my name on it, so she could recognize that I am me. That was all so complicated; who else would I be?"

"I'm not surprised she was suspicious of you, Hamilton," Adams remarked teasingly. "I've been suspicious about you, too.... But seriously, I do agree; it does all seem so complicated now."

Then, quickly changing the subject in the hope that Hamilton would choose not to respond to his jibe, Adams commented, "I heard they are all the way up to one hundred senators. That means there are fifty states now, all in our country...

"—and we saw that underground wagon to their office building, remember? The people called it a train. My God! And just why *are* those buildings so huge?

Jefferson chimed in with, "The members of The Congress must work a lot and produce many pages of legislation. I am impressed."

Washington, remembering looking out of the Capitol building toward the west, recalled seeing a mall at the end of the obelisk and a big memorial. He asked, "Did you know of this man? Abraham Lincoln? He must be younger than we all...."

"The residence areas in Philadelphia are beautiful and nice. Look at this." Jay changed the subject yet again, by pointing to a few houses on what appeared to be the main street outside of the business district. "I would love to live there. The comfort of living must be amazing. Did you mark the many wires all around? I heard that they transport something to the houses—electricity.... Wasn't old Ben Franklin the one who used to play around with lightning rods? Someone explained to me that, with electricity, you can heat, cook, and have light all at the same time. Astonishing to think that our Ben was the man who first brought the lights!"

Finally, Washington was growing weary of all the tumult that became Philadelphia...not to mention the conversation about how different, indeed, they were from their modern citizens.

"Come, let us talk of politics now," he requested, and all the others prepared to do so.

The Evening of November 3, 2020

George Washington, John Adams, Thomas Jefferson, and Alexander Hamilton meet on November 3, 2020, in Washington, D.C., at the Hay-Adams Hotel. They have drinks at the bar and watch the incoming results of the presidential election of that year. Prior to this year's election, the Founders had learned a great deal about American and world history over the last two hundred-plus years.

The president, who was elected in 2016, tried to get re-elected in 2020 and complained early on about how those "irregularities" were reducing his chances. The Founding Fathers watched the proceedings on a huge television screen hanging on the wall in the bar. For them, it was amazing to see so many different people talking, commenting about the incoming results. They were a little dizzied by all the activity going on around them. To steady themselves, they reflected on some basic rules they had used in 1789 and earlier.

~ ~ ~

John Adams opened: "It seems that the result will be quite narrow. It is the process we have designed that the Electoral College will eventually choose the president. So, it works!"

"Very interesting that the last time, in 2016, the president was elected by a majority of electoral votes but received fewer votes than his opponent, a woman, in the public vote. Very interesting," George Washington remarked.

"We wanted it that way back then," Alexander Hamilton reminded the first Father of the country, "We wanted to have the votes of the electors make the legitimate elections and not the votes of the people."

Thomas Jefferson cut in to say, "The reason for the Electoral College was because we did not trust the people enough not to be manipulated by public officers and intending presidents. Therefore, the Electoral College procedure is in fact a majority vote since it splits the direct vote into fractions. The majority of these fractions is crucial."

"Still, it's a bit strange that the will of the majority of voters isn't taken into account. I thought that the majority of votes would be decisive in determining the legitimacy of the elected president...." Adams nodded his agreement, with a bit of a hangdog look on his face.

Washington spoke next, "this does not mean the general election is useless. When people vote for their preferred candidates in general elections, they are actually voting for their electors—their state electors, to be precise. We also instituted the Electoral College to protect smaller states from having to suffer in silence in what was supposed to be a democracy. The most populous states cannot simply outvote the states with the lowest population numbers. It's a minority protection. Right?"

"The consequence of this has to be that most presidents feel cheated," Adams continued, "or at very least they'll think the system is slightly biased, since it is possible to win a general election and lose the Electoral College. That was what happened in the 2016 presidential election."

"Hmm, the 2016 thing is kind of weird," Hamilton pondered out loud. "I thought back then that such a split result could never happen—but it did happen with the very next election of you as president, John, in 1797—right out of the gate, as they say! Our principle that the small member states must be protected was not actually the problem at the time, with only thirteen states. There were probably smaller and larger numbers of inhabitants, which was expressed very strangely by the number of slaves. Since the black votes were not counted at that time, the legitimacy of those elected was not actually clear," he reminded them.

"Now I see the latest results for 2020 on the screen. It seems that the Democratic Party candidate is winning on both counts. That should bring a clear result," said Washington. "I'm curious to see how things will continue. It's almost midnight, the result is in, and the losing candidate is still making strange arguments that the election was stolen from him."

"He's been saying that for days, but as president and head of Administration, he should have to guarantee that the elections are conducted correctly," Hamilton reflected.

"We have invariably based ourselves on good faith, on ethical behavior. What we wanted was to build a strong republic that was not at the mercy of a king's whims," Washington stated, firmly.

"Our intention, after all, was to create a new country that would achieve through virtue a legitimacy that was unchallenged," he continued.

"It cannot be that the institutions of our new state—which are based on ethics and virtue—do not come into play. It is quite impossible that these elections are falsified on a large scale. So really..."

"Virtue, honesty, and sincere attitude were the mainsprings of the new land we dreamed of," Adams cut into Washington's reverie.

"But, what's the point of the losing candidate's chatter?" Washington asked. "What is he talking about? I cannot believe that American institutions do not function."

"We should remind all Americans, that we are a republic," Jefferson brought up. "We elect all our representatives for a designated period of time. That's it. They might be re-elected, or other candidates will be successfully elected to serve in their place. A certain number is not re-elected and must leave. That is clear, short, and simple."

"For us it is clear," Washington stated. "It's clear that the republic is contrary to a monarchy, where the rulers come out of a family or a family dynasty. That was exactly what we wanted to eliminate. We wanted to manage our business ourselves, contribute our ideas directly and not rely on a king and his 'noble' administrators. The defeated candidate of today does not seem to know these principles, or does not want to live and show them. He's acting like he owns the win. That's absurd. He is very old-fashioned. He reminds me of our age in the eighteenth century."

"I had heard that, in these days, the U.S. is a republic and not a democracy! That is nonsense," Hamilton demanded. "Republic and democratic rules belong together like two sides of a coin. Ruling a republic requires clear specifications and rules. All Americans must know and live these principles; they must adapt their inner attitudes and act accordingly."

"A republic can only function with democratic rules, in order to rule out arbitrariness and injustice on the part of those who are now in power, the politicians," Adams added his opinion. "That is very important and must still be valued in 2020!"

"If you gentlemen will recall," Jefferson reminded his colleagues, "we studied different cases of democracy. We learned about the details of Greek rules and the Roman institutions, checked the functioning of the Confederation of the Cantons in Switzerland, and the Dutch Republic, all to form an American way to rule our new country.

"Our three documents—the Declaration of Independence, the Constitution, and the Bill of Rights—are still impressive. Remember, we worked hard on the principles, and on many details, right? The intentions and values expressed in this package of noble aims are not exhausted and worn out—on the contrary, our spirit of that time seems to be fading. What a strange time I see today, in 2020."

"Remember the ideas of Montesquieu, who proposed the doctrine of Separation of Power by dividing the government into the executive, the legislation, and the judicial?" Hamilton reminded his colleagues. "What a historic step! My word!

"It is still, today, so fundamental for a republic that the power shall not be concentrated in one hand—as it was by James I at that time—but divided in sections and limited in time."

"The election process is a democratic basic principle." Adams took the floor for a moment. "There should be a wave of enthusiasm about attracting the highest number of participants. The higher, the better! Sadly, today I do not see any enthusiasm to let all the people who can join in the ballot boxes....

"It is my impression that today the opposite is true. With many states introducing electoral restrictions that make voting difficult, not at all easier. Did you, dear friends, read these political paths as well? Is anyone supposed to understand that? I certainly don't!"

"Don't they know that only the results of *fair* elections give those elected the authority to make decisions on behalf of the people?" Hamilton asked. "Only fair elections with a high participation allow the elected politicians to act in the name of the people."

"Bogus elections, with restrictions and obstacles, leave a stale aftertaste to many. How do people react? They turn away from politics," Washington threw his words out as if they hurt his mouth. "It would be very important that as many as possible are interested in the political world. After all, it will be their own world that they will be shaping and living in."

"The Constitution, with its amendments, is like the hardware," Hamilton said. "If the Constitution is the hardware of American democracy, the citizens' thinking, attitudes, and ideas about democracy are the software.

"So, I think the software of American democracy in 2020 is broken," he continued. "Many Americans today only understand democracy as the situation wherein their own party wins. That is strange and completely wrong. The decomposition of the democratic rules goes so far that only the advantages of one's own party are considered democratic. This is pure party politics, but it is not democracy."

"We can say a written Constitution is nice to have, but certainly it is not sufficient by itself," Adams replied, and then continued.

"And to be honest, a constitution is always incomplete. We understand that there are many interests, and they are subject to competing interpretations. At the time, we probably did not respect these changing interests enough. The system has been, for the last hundred years, subjected to special interests and not the will of the common people."

"What would we do differently today, my friends?" Washington challenged his old partners.

The Political Structure of America

An interesting aspect of America's political history is the different discoveries and interpretations the Founding Fathers' work has been subjected to over time. There is so much to examine in the history of America's political system—some have called these living documents, because they often undergo close scrutiny with every new era the country faces.

To be sure, America's political history is not a set of laid-down rules and regulations that collect dust on their shelves. Rather, they are routinely reviewed, re-thought, and often changed, rendering the system an ongoing method of the changes a democratic government must make to keep pace with its people.

There have been modifications. There have been errors. There has been deliberate tampering with the Constitution, overstepping and perhaps too much undermining and too many uncommunicated truths.

~~~

To a large extent, the work of the Founding Fathers has gone through many modifications since the years of their design. These modifications have huge, very significant to the development of America as a leading nation in the world. By now, you must be familiar with how the Founding Fathers revolted against British rule and fought for America's independence.

When we surf through history and sample the original intentions of the Founding Fathers, we tend to get blindsided as to how America evolved beyond its original intentions. It did not follow any pre-ordained pattern, but a dynamic structure. Not to get blindsided by this structure, here is the history as it might have been examined by the Founding Fathers, showing how the political structure of America may have been intended to work.

~ ~ ~

"There were thirteen colonies under British Rule, right?" John Adams asked rhetorically, when the group of old friends met in an espresso bar in Washington's Capitol district.

"Yes. But there was no specific decree that it had to be thirteen. For all he cared, King James I only wanted to colonize the coast of America within a certain latitude and longitude. This was around 1606," America's first president responded.

"But our history books say it was the eighteenth and nineteenth century," Alexander Hamilton reminded his colleagues, with an almost annoying conviction.

"Yes. That is not wrong," James Madison agreed. "The colonies were divided into thirteen during this period. But that was not King James' main concern. He only wanted to take hold of America as he did in other countries, through discoveries. He did this with the single intention of expanding the nation of Britain, which was fast becoming an empire."

"But was it Britain that helped America develop into the fifty-two states we have now?" Thomas Jefferson asked knowingly.

"Fifty," Hamilton corrected him swiftly.

Jefferson scoffed. "You know Puerto Ricans and constituents of the District of Columbia can't vote."

"The most amusing thing about America is its ability to thrive in the midst of chaos. Believe me, America is not the godliest of nations," Hamilton continued. "To a large extent, it has experienced a great deal of unexplainable growth and blessings in the past centuries."

"And by unexplainable growth, you mean slavery?" Adams asked with a squirm. "It's so funny how people are quick to agree that America thrives because it is 'God's own nation,'" Adams added sarcastically. "We just need to agree that slaves built this country. Period."

"Well, they didn't build everything," Jefferson noted.

"What? Did you just hear yourself?" Hamilton countered.

"Gentlemen! The reason we are having this discussion is to make you realize the truth about everything. You won't do that if you keep going at each other.

"So," Washington continued, "as I was saying, the colonies thrived despite many hardships and diseases. There were also many economic opportunities created by economic growth plans, which spurred on more interest in America, especially by the British government. King George believed America was the land he had been looking for, and he further strengthened his hold on the lands he colonized. Gradually, around the seventeenth century, America had expanded so much that there was a need to divide it into thirteen individual colonies, to make her management more effective."

"But why didn't America gain her Independence immediately after it expanded? I mean, it was getting powerful enough," John Jay stated sincerely.

"Please, never underestimate British Power," Washington articulated as if he was warning them to get ready to hear the worst. "The Britons had mastered the art of colonization more than any other nation in the world and seeing that America proved more productive than their other colonies, they had next to no intention of letting her go."

"Yeah, but I still don't understand how the colonies multiplied so much that they had to be divided into thirteen," Adams added his own thoughts, rather than asked.

"That's a smart observation, John," Washington agreed. "You see, since Britain observed America's geometric progression, they started allowing their citizens to immigrate to America so as to enjoy the many economic opportunities the young colonies provided. Obviously, people moved from Britain to America by the thousands."

"Voluntarily?" Hamilton asked.

"I'm getting to that," Washington said, and forced a wry smile. "Not everyone went voluntarily. America might have been developing, but Britain was far ahead of us at the time. No one wanted to leave their home for America; the very passage was treacherous. So, what the British government did was send political convicts and prisoners to America, as well as African slaves."

"Wait...what?" Madison was taken with surprise. "Slavery was brought about by British rule?"

"No," Hamilton burst in. "Slavery came to the shores of America before colonization, but we can say that colonization contributed greatly to it. About four hundred years ago, in 1619, some African slaves were brought to one of the colonies—Virginia, to be precise. To be honest, some documentation proves that it was even as early as the fifteenth century.

"At the time," he continued, "English people dominated America, but Africans were next in the majority. It was only during the eighteenth century that some German and Scottish people began to immigrate to some of the colonies. While the French and Spaniards were obsessed with other parts of America, Britain focused on the thirteen colonies: New Hampshire, Rhode Island, Maryland, Massachusetts, Georgia, Delaware, Connecticut, New York, Pennsylvania, New Jersey, Virginia, North Carolina, and South Carolina."

"So, they expanded to become fifty-two states, right?" Jefferson asked impatiently.

"Fifty," Hamilton corrected him again, and scoffed, assured he had belittled his old nemesis appropriately.

"The people who lived in the American colonies were more dependent on themselves than they were on Britain. This made them find an identity for themselves other than the identity Britain created for them. This is one of the reasons America forged ahead of Britain, and then all other nations in the world."

Washington cleared his throat, indicating he would take the floor. "We all know that, after the American Revolutionary War, the thirteen colony states became the original states of America and were admitted into the Union of American States through the Union of States' agreement. The

Articles of Confederation—the United States' first constitution—permitted the admission of new states into the new union, and gradually, thirty-eight more states were created following the clause in the Constitution. Some of these states were created through existing states that broke away from their original state through secession. *That* is amazing!"

"Like Maine from Massachusetts, and Kentucky from Virginia," Jay pointed out.

"And West Virginia from Virginia, because of the War of the States," Hamilton chimed in.

"Exactly," Washington affirmed. "These states are then further divided into counties, which are each also headed by a county executive, and in some cities also, by another leader known as mayor. A state can definitely have more than one county. In fact, there are over three thousand counties in America right now—*just unbelievable!*" he said.

"But Louisiana and Alaska use parishes and boroughs," Jefferson added, not to be drowned out by his peers, "and don't forget that New York City itself is divided into boroughs."

"Thomas, different names, same purposes. The purpose of a subdivision in a state is to manage the affairs of the people at the grassroots level. As long as this is done, it doesn't matter what name it is called." Adams basked in the acknowledgment of much shaking of heads in agreement around him. Those two were still second-guessing each other.

"But they are not sovereign," Jay observed, continuing.

"This is for the interest of the nation. If they were sovereign, there would be discrepancies in plans for a state, because different counties would want different things, and that would lead to so much confusion and no development. So yes, the counties have to be answerable."

"Sensible!" Adams commented, delighted to get the last word in as he continued to speak.

"At this point, you can then deduce that the governors head the states, and their administrations are fashioned after that of the federal government. I would not use the word *parodies* for their administrations, but they do help implement the decisions of America at the state level. For example, they approve state budgets and enact legislation."

"So, is that all about the political structure of America?" Hamilton asked.

"No, Alex," Washington smiled at his still-younger colleague. "This is only the beginning, and it's about to get even more interesting."

~ ~ ~

In the discourse between these gentlemen, we see that the political structure of America rests on its own evolution as a dominating country in the world. The amazing thing is that, although there are set patterns to enable these logistics, they are not rigid. Some states do not adopt certain patterns created for their functioning, although they adopt similar alternatives.

This goes to prove that while there are fifty states in America, things are not done one way in these fifty states. In fact, things may be done fifty ways in the fifty states. Look at Louisiana, whose laws do not follow any of those of the thirteen colonies, but the French, who founded that state. While they stay answerable to the White House, dynamism permits them some amount of autonomy where it is needed. This is because there are variations to the needs and developments of each state, and these needs are catered to with their specific variations.

"Why only two parties?"

Unlike most democratic nations in the world, America has had a two-party system since the beginning. This may be surprising to a lot of people, since America is considered to be one of the most democratic nations in the world. Why then, does a first-world country like the U.S. offer only two choices of party systems for their citizens? This question does not hang in the air, as you shall read in Washington's statement on this subject extensively, below.

~~~

"We, the Founding Fathers, again?" Thomas Jefferson asked this time while having a drink and some oysters at the Old Ebbitt Grill, at 15th Street NW in the new old capital.

"As I told you, we made some significant decisions for America, and while people are being affected by a few of those decisions, they are also reaping the benefits of the logical ones," George Washington responded.

"And having only a two-party system is logical?" Jefferson repeated.

"Well, that's why we are talking about it now," Washington answered. "The basic truth is that we, the Founding Fathers, did not create two-party systems for America. In fact, it is not specifically written in the Constitution that there must be only two political parties. It is easy to put another party onto the ballots with a few numbers of signatures. The United States is officially a multi-party system, though only two matter."

"Wait. Really?" Jefferson asked. "I thought you either had to be a Democrat or a Republican."

"No, Tom," Washington advised. "It doesn't have to be that way. It didn't even start with Democrats and Republicans. Those parties sprung up along the way. In our time, the two parties were the Federalist Party and the Democratic-Republican Party."

Hamilton, who would never be able to be president in any case because he was an immigrant, burst out laughing. "There was a Democratic-Republican Party? Right? America is such a joke."

"The Democratic-Republican Party was, in our time, referred to as the Anti-Federalists," Washington continued. "The party appealed to conservatism and business, favored centralization, modernization, federalism, and protectionism, while The Federalist Party favored agrarianism, republicanism, political equality, and expansionism. That was our world, and I recall we discussed all these details extensively." Washington was growing tired, but he was determined to make his points.

"As you know, the Democratic-Republican Party strongly opposed the Federalist Party and gained power over them. They were a very strong opposition, and gradually, the Federalist Party began to fade out of existence, especially since they didn't support the War of 1812, when America fought against Britain."

"Hmm...so which party replaced the Federalist Party? And why are there still only two parties?" John Jay asked.

"The Constitution does not spell out the existence of only two political parties in America. Still, the system seemed modified to work for only two political parties," Jefferson affirmed.

"Modified how?" Hamilton asked.

"The strongest two parties in the country are sufficient umbrellas for the majority of the people's interests. Of course, a third party has often arisen now and then. Still, since it contains a handful of people who know for sure they are not getting representation, it is only logical that they align with the interests of either of the other two political parties whose ideology is most similar to their own."

"So, there can be a third party?" Jefferson asked.

"Yes. But there is no point. Since two strong political parties are always formed over time in the country, their ideologies create so much friction that it becomes unnecessary when a third party comes with its own ideologies."

"Well, not unnecessary. Maybe just unimportant," Madison pointed out.

"Exactly," Washington confirmed. "Besides, we had no intention of creating a political party. You know, John, the first president of the United States was not elected through any political party. Our intention was that America would not be partisan, because we knew that would create so many factions. So, you see, we did our best for—us."

"And as you predicted, Mr. First President, factions sprang up first from us, the Founding Fathers," Adams said definitively, hoping they were wrapping up this particular conversation.

"True. From 1828 to 1854, two new political parties—although not entirely new—sprang up. The Whig Party, from the former Democratic-Republican Party, and the Democratic Party. The Democratic Party had the upper hand. Over time, 1854 to 1890 saw only the Democratic Party and Republican Party. But, honestly, since then, America's political system hasn't entirely evolved or changed drastically," Washington acknowledged.

"What about the independent or third-party systems?" Adams asked.

"One quite popular political party—besides the Democrats and Republicans—was the Anti-Masonic Party. It was more of a revolution than a party, though, probably because its main aim at the time of establishment was kicking against freemasonry. It folded, because of its lack of continued purpose," Jefferson chimed in.

Adams recalled, "Were they not the ones who joined the Whigs?"

"Yes," Washington confirmed.

Hamilton spoke next: "The individual or nonpartisan politicians had an even lesser upper hand, unless they were remarkable personalities who were already famous with the people. The only elected U.S. president without any political affiliations was you, George—who kicked against the idea anyway. No other independent president has been elected, and in my honest opinion, I don't think any other independent president can ever be elected in America."

"Let us never say never, gentlemen," Jay avowed, shaking his head with wonder.

"Hmm.... But in your defense, John," Washington added, "there have been many governors, representatives, and senators who were independently elected to office. Maine, Rhode Island, Texas, Alaska, Oregon, and Minnesota boast of them."

The noteworthy thing about America's party system is that the Founding Fathers tried as much as possible to establish an independent form of representation that proved successful without political affiliations—especially with the choice of George Washington being the first president of the United States of America. Diversities in opinions and ideologies were enough reasons to split into two different parties, and the amusing thing was, this split started with the Founding Fathers. First, they were divided into two main factions, which then turned into two political parties.

The argument, therefore, remains this: While trying to rule out the existence of a threat, the Founding Fathers did nothing to prevent the eventuality of that threat. Out of the many members of the different reunions to form the Declaration of Independence, the Constitution, and the Bill of Rights were the representatives of the two parties of the time. Within a few years of existence, there were partisan fights for power.

Therefore, if political parties had been created for the sole purpose of satisfying or representing people's opinions, America might not have had only two political systems as they do now. The Founding Fathers safely assumed that, as long as they were together under one umbrella, they could bring the country with them under that umbrella as well. What they didn't understand was that America is too big of a country to be sectionalized under one umbrella.

Unfortunately, there were, from the beginning, efforts to deliberately exclude some groups of voters. Today, subtle regulations are known, such as the opening times and locations of polling stations, the number of voting machines, the requirements for a voter ID with a photo, but also bans on offering food for those willing to vote, and in some states even for water as they wait in lines for hours. They lead to the fact that fewer Americans are going to the ballot box. These measures favor one party or the other, and party interests have evolved beyond the understanding of democratic principles.

The Impact of the American Constitution on Politics

"We the People of the United States, in order to form a more perfect Union, establish Justice, ensure domestic Tranquility, provide for the common defense, promote the general Welfare, and secure the Blessings of Liberty to ourselves and our Posterity, do ordain and establish this Constitution for the United States of America."

—Preamble, the American Constitution

The Constitution is regarded as one of the building blocks of American democracy. In fact, a lot of people believe that the Constitution is the bedrock on which America thrives. That's not wrong—and yet, there are still some additions to be made after all these many years.

To a certain extent, the Founding Fathers *fortified* the Constitution as best they could. They had the singular aim of making America as democratic as a country could ever be. This is why the first Constitution of America—the Articles of Confederation—gave more powers to the States that made up the federation, rather than the central government. The reason for this is because the Founding Fathers saw how very powerful Britain was at the central government, and they feared America would suffer the same fate and likely fail under the autocratic rule of some leader.

It is with this same conviction that the Constitution had to go through so many changes, especially with the incorporation of the Bill of Rights, the first ten amendments of the document.

To a certain degree, the Founding Fathers' efforts to fortify the Constitution have been misinterpreted by many people. Their erroneous belief is that the written Constitution is the sole provider of the democratic rules that guide the country.

The Constitution is the skeleton for a broader understanding of governing a country. It is the starting point for the American people to understand democratic rules that will enable them to guide their country through all that may arise. Countless events can spike up in the life of a country that are not clearly stated in its constitution. At best, many words may have been left vague deliberately—or left out completely—to act only as guidelines in different circumstances that could not have been anticipated at the start.

The complexity of any situation at hand is determined by what part of the Constitution is applied. If the complexity of the situation does not match any clause in the Constitution, the leaders must resort to being as democratic as they can be for the protection of America and its citizens.

To help with understanding the dynamics of the American Constitution, please follow the dialog below. The unknown neighbor wonders what the Constitution says in the likelihood that such an unfortunate event should occur.

~ ~ ~

George Washington was sitting in the kitchen of a house just off North Quincy Street in Arlington, Virginia. "No, Lenard, it just can't happen," Washington pronounced.

"But I have seen it in the movies," Lenard, Washington's nephew, told his uncle.

"Movies are not real-life events, Lenard," Washington responded.

"I get your point, Uncle. But don't be quick to rule mine out. It hasn't happened, but it can happen. What happens when someone attacks the White House?" Lenard asked.

"No one is going to attack the White House, Lenard."

"There are three movies about it! And they are perpetually looking for the president's son. So, what will happen to them? Do they go into some underground bunker, or through a wall? Will you offer yourself up as a sacrifice for the American people like you, President Washington, did in *Olympus Has Fallen?*"

"No. No. No and no. God forbid. But if such things were to happen, there is a Security Council, and a state of emergency will be declared."

"Okay. But then who would handle the attackers?"

"I can't believe I am answering these questions," Washington muttered and then smiled at his very curious nephew. "The Army. They are charged with defending America, and that is exactly what they would do."

"But what if the attackers are already inside the White House and the Security Council are given an ultimatum, or else they will kill the president?" Lenard asked.

"Well, the Security Council finds a way around it," Washington informed him.

"But that is so vague. Does the Constitution not specifically say what to do about such things?" Lenard asked, genuinely inquisitive.

"Well, it does say to declare a state of emergency. But I'm afraid it doesn't say specifically how to handle the situation."

"So, anyone can do anything?" Lenard asked innocently.

"No, Lenard. It is not as simple as that. See, when I was to be sworn in as president of the United States of America, I swore an oath to put America first, to protect America. This means I must do that regardless of how my own family or I myself fare."

"No," Lenard replied. "But what you did say that day was 'I do solemnly swear that I will faithfully execute the Office of President of the United States, and will, to the best of my ability, preserve, protect, and defend the Constitution of the United States.' So, you promised to defend the American Constitution, not the people of America."

"What? No. How do you even remember my oath? Lenard, what you don't understand is that the Constitution of America establishes the protection of its citizens. So, if I protect the Constitution, I am also protecting the American people. Now, Lenard, we have to stop talking about attacks on the White House," Washington cautioned.

"I understand. But what you just made me realize is that there are loopholes in the American Constitution. Uncle, do you want to tell me that all parts of the Constitution protect the American citizens as much as they should? The implication of that oath is that there are parts of the Constitution that will need to be protected, but that do not put the people first. In fact, the Constitution comes first, before the people, and that leaves a lot of questions hanging in the air."

Washington was silent for some seconds after Lenard spoke. Then he said, "You know what? Lenard, you are right. The American Constitution does not say it all. Basically, all it does is point us the way, and as people who have been chosen to protect the Constitution, I can only make some additions and changes along the way. I don't interpret the Constitution; the Judiciary does," Washington declared conclusively.

"Yes, but isn't that subject to the discretion and sometimes the bias of a judge? Yes, the Constitution says to punish criminal offenders, but it doesn't specifically say for how many years they should be punished.

"Lenard, I won't tell you that there is no corruption in America. But as much as possible, we try to do our best with what the Constitution says."

"I know that," Lenard said. "But I'm trying to say that the Constitution is not actually enough to ensure democracy in this country. Suppose the interpretation of the Constitution is still subject to the persons who make up the Judiciary. Then there will definitely be some errors that contravene what the Constitution requires."

"Errors? What are you talking about, Lenard?"

"Okay, Uncle. Look at the infamous Central Park Jogger Case in 1989. The convicts were Black and Latino youths who were sent to jail for six to twelve years because they were 'criminal offenders,' when we know deep down that the only reason the judge was so willing to send them to jail was because they were not White."

Washington sighed heavily. Lenard continued.

"Benjamin—my classmate—told me that his distant cousin, who is Black, was caught with a gentleman's amount of cocaine and was sent to five years in prison. Around the same time, his White friend who was going to make the same delivery was caught and given two years with parole. So, who are we kidding, Uncle?"

Washington forced a smile. "Lenard, I am glad that you see through America. But like I told you, the Constitution, no matter how much of an ideal it is to us, is still subject to our actions and decisions. As a country, we can only pray and hope to have the right leaders who are willing to align themselves with the guidance of the Constitution." Washington spoke gently to his nephew.

"Right, leaders like you," Lenard stated, grinning from ear to ear.

Washington smiled and nodded, then hugged his nephew.

~ ~ ~

In his own little innocent and spirited way, Lenard was trying to clear some cobwebs about the "inefficiency" of the American Constitution, and why it is still subject to a great amount of flexibility even in the hands of those who are supposed to interpret and protect its clauses. Apparently, as it stands, there are gaps and inconsistencies in the application of the Constitution.

In fact, these "gaps and inconsistencies" come when human emotions, intellect, and bias have to be employed in the process of application. While there are some noteworthy efforts made to enhance democratic principles in America—

as the Founding Fathers attempted throughout their lifetimes—the country has had its fair share of democratic wrongs.

For example, when we examine what a "constitutional crisis" is, the Constitution does not clearly define when a crisis has occurred in the process of its application. The closest inkling may be that it's a violation of the rule of law and the dictates of the Constitution. This may still be wrong as well because a constitutional crisis can arise when a country's political system is working as perfectly as it should.

Even if the country's political system is not working as it should, because there are no ways to solve any particular crisis, more questions begin to arise as to whether any crisis has occurred in the first place. The Constitution does not explicitly state what is or what is not a constitutional crisis.

The Role of America's Constitution in Political Parties

"Partisan politics bears the imprimatur only of tradition, not the Constitution."

—The Supreme Court, Elrod v. Burns (1976)

The Founding Fathers never intended that politics in America would be partisan. As much as they would have liked, or as they thought it should be, individual representations should be enough to keep contentions of any kind away from America.

Unfortunately, this sole belief was not enough to keep political parties away from America. Even though George Washington was the first president and became president without the help of any political party—there were no political parties at that time—all it took was one different political ideology and Washington's plan would have been upended. Political parties would come to thrive in America shortly after Washington's election, and with their accompanying ideologies they would come to stay permanently.

As the Supreme Court spoke of partisan politics in that quotation above, the Founding Fathers' lack of belief in political parties caused them to avoid creating any parties. Nor did they encourage anyone else to establish or enable the growth of party systems in America. In that climate, you would guess right that the Constitution does not specify any party system. Maybe they were right, but the political party system is an embedded "tradition" nevertheless.

American historian Clinton Rossiter wrote that, "No America without democracy, no democracy without politics, no politics without parties, no parties without compromise and moderation." As controversial as this statement may appear, it contains some quantity of truth. Political parties may have caused some uprisings in America, as they are especially good at dividing the people based on political views. Still, the party does give people some amount of fixed knowledge about the work to be done by any political figure.

As these parties clash in ideas, inquisitive Lenard cannot but wonder whether the American Constitution has played a role in contributing to many uprisings that have come to the fore throughout the nation's history. Let's listen in...

~ ~ ~

"Is it not because there is no part in the Constitution that recognizes political parties, that the political parties hate each other so much?" Lenard asked while sipping a milkshake in the kitchen of his parents' house.

"No, Lenard," his Uncle George had to disagree. "The Constitution does not recognize political parties, but that is not why political parties are at each other's throats."

"So, you agree," Lenard stated.

"That?" Washington asked and poured himself a glass of water.

"Political parties are at each other's throats."

"No, Lenard, I have many friends in both the Democratic and Republican parties," Washington responded firmly.

"A few?" Lenard asked sarcastically.

Washington sighed. "Few. Look, Lenard, while I agree with you that political parties are definitely not friends with each other, I wouldn't call us enemies either. The Constitution may not recognize them, but there is some unspoken civility between them."

"Unspoken civility?" Lenard asked, raising his eyebrows.

"There are rules of mutual tolerance and forbearance. And before you ask, mutual tolerance is understood as an act of dislike or disagreement, but each accepts the other as legitimate."

"But that still does not rule out the concept of enmity between the parties."

"Len, I don't think it's possible for you to understand someone you do not share ideological differences with."

"Which is what we have in America," Lenard declared, conclusively.

"Kind of. You just have to realize that the other party member is not your enemy. You know, there is this comment by Levitsky & Ziblatt that says, 'Mutual toleration is politicians' collective willingness to agree to disagree.' That is a correct statement," Washington agreed, emphatically. "Today, in 2020, it does not seem to be true."

"Who are Levitsky & Ziblatt?" Lenard asked.

Washington laughed. "That's not the point. The point is that political parties understand that the unity of America comes first before anything else. If what we are truly fighting for is the installment of a good leader in America, then we need to understand the importance of unity," he continued, trying to sound as exhaustive as possible.

"But that is not what political parties are fighting for. They are not fighting for the installment of good leaders. They are fighting for control of power," Lenard commented calmly.

"Smart," Washington complimented his nephew. "But I want you to know that it is not as simple as assuming that America's political parties operate as they like or only to control power. There are rules that guide them even if they are not specifically recognized by the Constitution. And as far as power control goes, that is something we don't have control over automatically. No one rules for as long as they want to, and whether you like it or not, if you are a bad leader, the American citizens will not vote for you twice."

"But that stands to be corrected. Because 'bad' is subjective," Lenard countered. "There are loads of people today who claim that Donald Trump is the best president America ever had."

At that, Washington laughed heartily. "See, Len. I want you now, in 2020, to remove the phrase 'enmity' from the two political parties in America and substitute it with 'agree to disagree.' There are other problems that America faces that are bigger than political parties. Problems like partisan politics are the least of our worries. We face constant security threats all the time, and these threats do not care who belongs to what political party, which is why we must stand together and combat these threats. A way out of the deadlock would certainly be to focus on factual issues and find possible common ground for improvements—that is everyday politics."

~ ~ ~

Lenard's intention is not to come to a quick conclusion that partisan politics are the root problem of politics in America. To him, it seems the simplest explanation, but there is a basic truth: partisan politics has never been the root of America's political problems. True, they are a factor, but they are not the root.

America faced political problems way before political parties came onto the political scene, and there have been quite a few uprisings with political parties. However, as Washington knew well, there are rules, no matter how unspoken they are, that have guided the conduct of political parties. These rules prevent whatever "uprising" might be going on with the political parties. So yes, Washington established that there are disagreements between the two political parties, but America has much bigger fish to fry.

Voting Rights

Without a doubt, voting plays a critical part in the democratic process of any nation. Indeed, it is the citizens' right to vote in a free and fair process that separates democracy from autocracy. In fact, it is widely referred to as the most important single factor in electing leaders in the free world.

While much attention is paid to respecting the process, little attention is paid to retaining the originality of the process itself. Instead, it seems America has become more concerned about the fact that it allows the populace the "opportunity" of a general election. The Electoral College procedure shows a distrust toward the voters as it doesn't really approve, nor trust, the people's wishes. The list of problems goes on with the two-party system and its primaries, which favor extreme candidates. It is a fact that in 2021 und 2022 four hundred anti-voter bills had been approved in forty-eight U.S. states. These bills named unnecessary barriers for people to register to vote, vote by mail, or vote in person. Finally, there is gerrymandering, redrawing voting districts to ensure that a minority of voters will get a majority of seats.

Sad to say, the nation whose Founding Fathers searched high and low to find the best means of ensuring equality in their new nation is now in critical need of revisiting. Objectively, the methods being adopted in voting in the American system are capable of defeating the purpose of voting itself, and with this in mind these conversations were written, to examine the methods.

Furthermore, after conducting the necessary evaluation of America's voting methods, this text will also suggest alternative ways voting might be done in America. The true purpose of voting in America is in desperate need of attention if the country is to continue to prove how "exalted" it is in democracy.

As conversations highlight these alternatives, you will be offered an opportunity to learn, relearn, and unlearn things about history that you may have never heard or considered before. You will also be confronted with a view of history from an objective and analytic point of view, so that you may be empowered to formulate your own interpretation rather than be reduced to blind acceptance of the views of others.

America's Voting Process

Two things determine the credibility of any process charged with selecting the leaders of any nation, state, county, and city: first the people's choice, and second, a system that supports the people's choice. This is extremely important, as the rights of the people are ceded to the deputies. They make decisions on behalf of the people. If either of these voting details is not established in clear terms, or is partly adhered to, different kinds of agitations will spring up about the voting process.

In this case, confidence in the election process is dwindling—an extremely dangerous movement is emerging. Doubt and misgivings are spreading. This undermines the credibility of the legislator. The Founding Fathers were very concerned about this critical point.

America's voting process reflects this doubt today. The general election is the popular vote where everyone of a certain age, who is a citizen of the United States of America, can vote. Unfortunately, winning the popular vote does not mean you get to be president. The Founding Fathers, for fear that the populace would be manipulated by a desperate, obnoxious politician, set up a separate process, which would elect the president: It is called the Electoral College. To confuse matters further, the Electoral College is not a college at all. It is a group of voters who come together to vote a second time for the person they feel should be president.

George Washington was elected president by the Electoral College in 1789 and in 1793 without popular vote. His charisma as a victorious general in the American Revolutionary War made him the perfect politician to play a role model in many details as president of the newly founded State.

His vice president, John Adams, campaigned for the presidency in 1796, followed by a general election that took place from November 4 to December 7. It was the first time that political parties were dominant and supported their candidates.

Adams won with seventy-one electoral votes to the seventy votes for his competitor, Thomas Jefferson. It was the only time in U.S. history that the president and vice president belonged to different parties. Adams was a member of the Federalist Party; Jefferson was from the Democratic-Republican Party.

Let's continue to participate in the discussion that took place in spring 2021 in Alexandria, Virginia, presumably at The Majestic on King Street.

∼ ∼ ∼

"For a long time, we have been struggling to ensure that those entitled to vote are represented as fairly as possible. Yet, we invented the Electoral College. Does that mean the popular vote is just an empty democratic show?" Alexander Hamilton asked, with concern.

"No. The popular vote is useful, although not as important as the Electoral College. To get the chance to be voted for by the Electoral College, you must have a percentage of votes in the general election," George Washington answered.

"Right.... Okay, didn't we think those 'qualified individuals' of the Electoral College would be even easier to manipulate than a whole populace?" John Adams asked.

"Intelligent question, John," Washington complimented the second American president, and grinned. "Which then brings us to the next thing about America's voting process—the concept of gerrymandering."

"Wait...are you for real? Gerrymandering? What is that?" Hamilton asked.

"America is not a saint country, Alexander. We have our many flaws, and unfortunately, gerrymandering sticks to us like bees to nectars," Washington concluded.

"What is gerrymandering?" Hamilton asked again, sincerely.

Adams rolled his eyes.

"It's when someone decides to manipulate an electoral constituency by means of geography, so it can favor his party, or some class of people, and cause him to win the election," Adams affirmed, thoroughly but impatiently.

"Yes. Thank you for that explanatory definition, John," Washington approved, "but that is just a textbook definition of gerrymandering. Gerrymandering started with an American politician who was, in fact, the fifth vice president of the United States—Elbridge Gerry. We knew him personally as a member of the Massachusetts delegation to the Constitutional Convention in Philadelphia. The term 'gerrymandering' was named after him."

"No way!" Adams proclaimed. "Looks like we did our own share of democratic tweaking."

"We were and we are human, John," Washington reminded his old friend, while giving Adams the side-eye. "At that time, Gerry was the Governor of Massachusetts. He had earnestly worked for America. In fact, he was proven to be an honest politician."

"So, what happened to him?" Hamilton asked.

"Careful, Alexander, don't be so quick to judge," Washington warned. "Elbridge Gerry did his best for America. He was even one of the Fathers who refused to sign the Constitution at first, because it did not have a Bill of Rights. He very much believed in the liberties of the people and the state, until he did something that contradicted his stance."

"Gerry gerrymandered," Thomas Jefferson joked, and Washington laughed heartily.

"You see, at the time, Elbridge Gerry was a Democratic-Republican. In 1812, he passed a bill in the Massachusetts legislature that supported the creation of a partisan geographical district in Boston that favored the Democratic-Republican Party. The possible party votes are tracked down and added up in a district in such a way that a desired majority is formed. The district was created in South Essex,

Massachusetts. It was a disaster. People compared the new district creation to the picture of a salamander."

"Hmmm...Gerry Salamander. Gerrymander," Jefferson joked again.

"You are having fun with this, Tom, aren't you?" Hamilton asked.

Washington laughed again. "Yes. We are learning, but this is still supposed to be fun."

"Please continue," Adams asked impatiently.

Washington obliged. "This kind of activity, done by one of ours, gave headway to certain politicians to do the same thing, to favor their party when they were in the majority. It is considered undemocratic and even corrupt, but politicians have found a way around it to evade its illegality. This is why it was not surprising that, some years later, words like Henry-mandering, Jerrymander, and Tullymander were named after politicians who had done what Elbridge Gerry did."

"Well, did he win the election?" Hamilton asked.

"No. He did not. People obviously knew what he did, and that was enough to make them lose their belief in him."

"But he was still chosen to run as vice president, wasn't he?" Adams observed.

"See? That's the difference between the people's choice and the system's choice. The people rejected Elbridge Gerry for his selfish decision of gerrymandering in the popular election, but the system embraced him through the Electoral College and installed him as vice president to James Madison," Washington reminded his colleagues.

"But was he a bad person?" Jefferson asked.

"Tom. America's voting system is not about Elbridge Gerry. Of course, we have our issues with the voting system, and occasionally, gerrymandering rears its head to characterize our electoral process."

"There are still constituency changes, which in the U.S. are called gerrymandering. So then, how do they do it?" Adams asked.

"See? That's what you are not getting, John," Washington responded. "Gerrymandering is about the manipulation of a geographical district to gain voting power. Elbridge Gerry did one style of gerrymandering, which means there are other methods to gerrymandering a voting process. The fact that Elbridge Gerry's legislature created another district doesn't mean that is the only way."

"Besides. His was obvious. We don't know what kind of subtle gerrymandering politicians do nowadays," Hamilton observed.

"Well, that is not very true. There is a census every ten years in each state. As the total number of representatives in the House remains stable, the population may vary. Therefore, the number of representatives to each state can change and that is the moment the state legislators may redraw the map. That is, today, common practice," Adams responded.

"The fact remains that gerrymandering realizes the intention that a minority of voters will obtain a majority of seats," Washington declared, in closing.

~~~

The truth is that America's voting system has its irregularities. But because the system is already programmed to work in such obvious obscurity—yes, the Electoral College—there might be subtle modifications that influence the supposedly perfect American voting process. It just matters who gets caught. As long as politicians play it safe and don't get caught, the process seems fair to people. After all, the popular vote has never been the ultimate decision. It's the reason people go to the polls to vote. In the best of times, we feel we put our best candidate in office.

Justifiable?

"Let each citizen remember at the moment he is offering his vote that he is not making a present or a compliment to please an individual; but that he is executing one of the most solemn trusts in human society for which he is accountable to God and his country."

Samuel Adams (second cousin of John Adams)

To date, in America, voting has been seen as the most imperative part of the democratic process. This is because the people believe in the power of voting and how it is able to change the narrative for the country, especially for the subjugated people of the country—the minorities, the people who don't have everything working for them as it does for others, like African Americans.

It is with the hope of continued growth and progress that the American people motivate each other to cast their votes regardless of their feelings. In fact, casting one's vote is an expression of responsibility for one's country, which allows—indeed, requires—every individual of a certain age to hold their leaders accountable, directly. Voting indicates a tremendous amount of trust on the part of the people, a significant investment in putting them in office. This is exactly why a famous American personality—George Carlin, the famous comedian—said, "If you don't vote, you lose the right to complain."

Agreed, the American people are implored to take voting seriously because their decisions and indecisions can either make, or not, their own chances for growth. What happens when there seems to be no motivating factors to inspire the people to vote—especially new voters, who are just coming of voting age? As we find out whether these excuses are justifiable, a father explains to his young son and daughter, who have just come to voting age, why it is so important for them to vote.

~ ~ ~

"My mind is made up, Dad. The only reason I'll vote is if they share Mexican Truffle Fries at the polls," Jim joked, grinning.

"And not just any Mexican Truffle Fries, the ones from *Camilla*. She makes them perfect," Jim's sister, Serena, chimed in. Serena and Jim did a high-five and giggled.

"How is it that you guys don't get it? Voting is the most important thing that reinforces democracy in America," their weary dad responded. "It's what proves that we get a voice no matter what society does or says," Mr. William Lee, George Washington's manservant from back then, brought up, with a high-pitched, concerned voice.

"Dad. You are overreacting. It's only two votes. It isn't going to change who becomes president or not," Serena told her father.

"That mentality is what put Donald Trump in office!" Will Lee exclaimed.

"There are worse presidents than Donald Trump," Jim said.

"Well, I don't think Donald Trump was a bad or worse president. If anything, he tried his best for America," Serena argued.

William Lee was having none of it. "Do you understand why voting is of particular importance to our people, and why we make it a point of duty to protect the interests of our race? Together, we worked to put Barack Obama, the first Black U.S. president in office—twice. "

"After 145 years of freedom?" Jim asked. "How is that a win?"

Lee shook his head. "Our forefathers were slaves for four hundred years, Jim, and we couldn't vote until 1867. That vote, as singular as it was, represented the significance of Black people to American history. But this isn't even about race or Black people! The vote of each American citizen represents their significance to America and America's significance to them. If you guys choose not to vote, then it only means that America is not significant to you!"

"Okay...that is not entirely deductive logic," Serena told her father.

"Don't you guys get it? Voting is what shows that we are ready and willing to support this country no matter what it takes. The good roads you play on every day; the nice house you sleep in, and you, Serena—the scholarship you just got offered from Stanford. Jim, the paid internship you got with *Teen Vogue*. All these represent opportunities that are available in this country because of the leaders we have," their father declared.

"Okay, now that *is* inductive logic. You know America is a capitalist country, right? So, if you are implying that there are economic opportunities because of our leaders, you are just so wrong," Serena remarked. "I got my scholarship because I worked hard for it, and I'm an athlete. I have a 4.0 CGPA, and I am a badass at women's football. Barack Obama did not do that for me."

"You know what, you are right," Mr. Lee agreed, and sighed. "But all I'm trying to say is that this country creates more and better products than comparable countries in the world because our leaders are reformative enough to invest their time and make precise decisions toward the furtherance of our nation. Any slight mistake in electing the wrong person could pull all this down in a heartbeat. How would you go to Stanford with your hard-earned scholarship if America became a war country? Or you, Jim, how would you design mind-blowing fashion looks and be credited for them if the odds were stacked against you as a Black person?"

Serena and Jim went silent for a few moments.

"I know you see things that don't impress you in this country. But it's all a process, and we are working toward ensuring that the process yields substantial results. We cannot do that without every single person's involvement," Lee emphasized.

"Well, Dad, I am trying to agree with you. I strongly believe that voting is significant for every person in America—especially people of other races. But like Herbert Marcuse wrote, 'Free election of masters does not abolish the masters or the slaves,'" Jim exclaimed.

"That is exactly why we need to have accountability, son. Herbert Marcuse was not a slave for one day in his life, so comparing representative government and the relationship between citizens and their leaders as slavery is myopic. These people represent us because we believe they can. And the best way to ensure that we are not subject to a parody of slavery is to make sure that we vote."

"Agreed," his son affirmed his father's words. "Voting is important. But we have questions to ask you."

～～～

At this point, Serena and Jim are gaining insight into the essence of voting for all the American people, especially the minority or people of other races. It is not just their constitutional right; it is something that gives them the power to voice their opinions and feelings.

Even as William Lee gets them to agree that voting is important, and he helps them see his reasons, Serena and Jim are ready to establish some things that will make their father rethink his stance. Hopefully, he will not lose the lesson he is trying to teach his young adult children about voting in America, in the process.

The Struggle Is Real

"Elections belong to the people. It's their decision. If they decide to turn their back on the fire and burn their behinds, then they will just have to sit on their blisters."
—Abraham Lincoln

Truer words have never been spoken and it is important to note that people do not just turn their backs to something they are somewhat sure will determine their progress as a nation. While it is true that some people—like Serena and Jim—are apathetic voters because they don't believe in the system, making them believe in the system, and the power of voting, is the most crucial thing, right?

That turns out not to be true. There are so many challenges associated with voting that it is enough to spur whatever apathy a voter might have, especially if the voter has no strong belief in the system at all, as is the case for Jim and Serena. Sometimes the conditions that surround the process of voting are so stringent that all sense of constitutional and moral duties to the country is suspended. But, to what extent are we willing to go, and what are the assurances that these challenges will be solved?

Things are about to get even more interesting....

~ ~ ~

"So yes, it is true that our being apathetic toward voting does not help our people or America...but, Dad, you have to agree that the odds are stacked against us so much that we think of voting as putting a horse through the eye of a needle," Jim remarked.

"What? What odds?" William Lee asked knowingly.

"Let us start from the fact that the distance between the houses of potential voters and their assigned polling booths is just too much. Last time, your voting location was sixty miles from here. You guys had to drive for three hours and we were worried about you," Serena said.

"Yeah, I remember," Jim replied, getting up to take something from the fridge.

"Dad, you must agree that the distance doesn't help the average voters. Especially people who are just of voting age. You can pick on us all you like, but why do I now have to drive extra far to vote?" Serena dared. "I don't even have a car!"

"Yes. But these challenges are not enough for the...."

"Importance of voting," Jim interjected. "Yes, we get it. But you have to admit that people who are just of voting age will find the distance a complete turn-off, especially if they have no strong affection for the process itself. In Georgia there is only one polling station in a large rural area. In Texas it is a known tactic of the GOP to rearrange the locations of the polling stations according to party preferences. Besides, many parents from school didn't go during that time because it coincided with our school anniversary."

"That was supposed to have been canceled," Mr. Lee protested. "But we can't deny that there are so many challenges the electoral body faces that, yes, it does make it hard for them to organize the election as perfectly as people might want it to be."

"Oh...tell the truth and shame the devil, father!" Serena glared at her father. "You know those challenges are more artificial than natural. The system is rigged against us, Dad. They deliberately put those things in place, so we don't get to vote. We all know it depends on what the Electoral College says."

"But the general election matters, too!" Mr. Lee brought up, rather defensively.

"Does it, though? Because it doesn't feel like it. The one time I wanted an American female president—and in fact, the majority of voters chose her, but the rules of the Electoral College elected someone else as president."

"Okay, I didn't like Donald Trump, but I don't think anything shady happened," Mr. Lee uttered, in nearly a whisper.

"'Cause you were there?" Jim asked. "See, Dad, no one knows for sure. We are all just playing a game of pretending that America's voting system is not messed up. We're trying to encourage ourselves to vote as if that is what matters by a hundred percent."

"It's not as simple as that, son," his dad promised, running out of words.

"If we wanted to make it easier for everyone, why is it that voting by mail only works in thirty-three out of the fifty states that America has?" Jim asked.

"And by works you mean it is riddled by crippling restrictions, right?" Serena supported her brother.

"Okay, that was relaxed during the Covid period," Mr. Lee chimed in quickly.

"Because there was a worldwide contagion," Serena reminded her father, with surprise. "How many contagions do we need to have before voting by mail is taken more seriously? Do you know how convenient it is to support voting by mail and make it a default form of voting in America? People are so obsessed with voting at the polls that they don't see how voting by mail is the future of voting. And e-voting is even more so."

"Because it is riskier than in-person voting. Everyone knows that!" Mr. Lee said.

"Yes. But has anything been done to eliminate that supposed problem? And do you think in-person voting cannot and has not been rigged in America?" Serena asked.

"Well, it's harder to rig," Mr. Lee admitted, feeling, suddenly, even more defensive.

"Oh my God, Dad. You know voting by mail will encourage more voter participation. The political establishment fears that, and they leave it to be. They argue it is a risk to change something. Doing nothing is in their favor - therefore no improvement of form of voting.," Jim articulated, showing his building frustration.

"And how would you improve it?" Mr. Lee fired back. "You know, we leave so much to our leaders that we bask in the fantasy that all problems can be solved with the snap of a finger. So, tell me, how would you improve it?"

"Well, for starters," Jim began, "I would emphasize the importance of voting by mail and how it can enhance voter participation. Then, I will make sure that those who want to vote by mail will do so during a specific time frame—preferably two weeks before the elections. After that, I will put in place tight security and an efficient process to ensure that people's votes are protected, and the integrity of the voting system is maintained. That way, people can and will be able to vote regardless of hindrances like distance, work, family, or transportation."

With that, William Lee went silent for a few seconds, before saying anything else. When he finally spoke again, it was to say, "It's hard to admit, but you are right."

~ ~ ~

To an extent, having William Lee admit that the voting system of America does not fully support voter participation is one of the most significant parts of their conversation. Here, Mr. Lee represents the system. People who are in the system regularly put-up excuses and have ready-made "diplomatic" answers and reasons as to why there are conditions that restrict voter participation. Serena lays it bare for him to see that these problems—which have been portrayed as insurmountable—can be solved in the most feasible ways possible.

The American voting system is subject to such challenges that it becomes almost impossible to be a fan of voting—apart from those who understand the duty behind it. But even some who do understand the duty behind it have commitments that are just too important to neglect for the sake of voting. Therefore, the argument stands that America does not support her citizens when it comes to voting, even though her citizens are ready and willing to vote.

It becomes essential to understand that incentivizing voting is not the goal; making voting more accessible to the populace *is*. The painful truth is that the challenges surrounding the process of voting itself seem more artificial than natural. It would be outright understandable if the system faced challenges that seem to be created by the hectic process of voting, and not challenges that seem as if they should not have occurred in the first place. As it stands, they appear to have been orchestrated. There is nothing wrong with putting voters near their homes, as this will make it more convenient for them to vote for the leader of their choice.

Meanwhile, even after agreeing to the fact that these challenges can be solved, Mr. Lee has yet to agree that the system itself creates all the challenges facing them now.

~ ~ ~

"Even if the polls are beside people's houses, they still won't vote!" William Lee shouted, throwing his hands in the air expressively.

"You can't take it with you, Dad," Jim remarked. "There are people who simply don't believe in the system anymore because the same thing keeps happening with the same president."

"What do you mean the same thing?" Mr. Lee asked.

"Okay, think of it. When Barack Obama became president, people—Black people, to be precise—were overjoyed that things were about to change for them. And so were other races; there was a ray of hope that things would change for them, too." Jim started.

"And it did!" his father said, conclusively.

"Did it, though?" Jim asked. "I had a Mexican friend, then, who said his mom wished there would be fair labor wages for Mexicans when Barack became president, since it was apparent that he would understand the wishes of the minority. But after eight years, she saw that nothing was changed; after that, it was exactly the same. Now, they don't vote in their family, and I don't blame them."

"Well, that's the way the society has been programmed! It was not and cannot be Barack Obama's fault. It's always been the White people, the Black people, the Latinos, and then all the other races. Do you think being a Black man and spending eight years in office is enough time to upend America's race and discrimination history?" Will Lee asked.

"I admit, you have a solid point, Dad. But it doesn't take away the fact that the minorities are neglected when it comes to planning, and their apathy is justified," Jim said. "Studies show that minorities are much more likely to live next to factories and other sources of pollution. Try building a steel plant next to a wealthy suburb. In inner cities, many people don't have access to grocery stores and fresh-food markets—just dollar stores, liquor stores, and fast-food restaurants.

"It's not even about minorities alone. There are some people—or should I say White people—who don't vote because they know that the system will always work for them no matter who becomes president," Serena commented.

"Okay, that's insensitive, because there are poor White people," Mr. Lee interrupted his daughter.

"—who still have their privileges no matter what," Serena remarked.

"What?" William Lee asked. "That does not sound right."

"Yes. It doesn't sound right because it is what it is. But, as you remarked earlier, that is the way our society has been programmed, and whether we like it or not, it affects voting," Serena countered. "Do you think I would want to vote if I knew that I would be seen as better than all other races in my country because of the color of my skin, and that no matter who becomes president, my privilege is intact?"

"Okay. Voting is larger than the race issue," Mr. Lee declared.

"Except it's not. The knowledge of their privilege is embedded in their consciousness, and it can impair their interest in voting," Serena said.

"Well, I know a ton of White people who vote," Will Lee promised.

"Again. Agreed. But can we dial it back to agree that, if the country should make plans toward enhanced voter participation, it could make the day of the elections a day off for everyone in the country or choose a weekend for elections. That way, easy access to the ballot boxes can be guaranteed, and people will have no excuse not to vote. Even me; I would take America seriously then, and vote," Jim answered.

"That's a strong point, Jim. See, I agree with that," his father acknowledged, nodding. Then he glanced at Serena with a searching face. "You don't agree?"

"Actually, I do," Serena answered. "Jim made a good point."

"But?" he persisted.

"But that is not all there is to improve! Some details of voting are not standardized, and this creates so much confusion for people. The one thing America seems to be good at is organization. But when it comes to voting and its processes, we are as bad as any other third-world country," Serena said.

"And what else needs to be standardized?" Mr. Lee asked.

"Oh...come on, Dad. There are no uniform opening hours at the polling booth, and that is so frustrating," Jim barked. "The day you and Mom drove a hundred miles to vote, you got there only to realize that the opening hours were four hours before you got there, and the booth was almost closed. So, you had to sleep in a stranger's house that night, and we were concerned about you all the way until you got back home."

"Okay, the Kellys were not strangers. Unfortunately, we became attached to the polling booths and some facilities. But you do have a solid point. America does mess up the opening hours for voting. But that doesn't happen every time, and I don't think that should be enough reason to discourage anyone from voting," her father brought up.

"It is," Serena agreed and raised her eyebrows. "For me it turns out that the elections should begin with the dispatch of the voter ID cards by a local authority."

"What? You advocate for voter participation and say there should be resident control?" Mr. Lee asked, genuinely confused.

"No, Dad, that's not what I am saying." Now it was Serena's turn to be frustrated.

"I believe what Serena means is that suffrage ID cards with photos should be provided to everyone in all states, so the integrity of the electoral process can be protected," now it was Jim's turn to support his sister. "People should use official documents, like their driver's licenses or other major documents, that show their photos and attest that it's really them."

"And is there a reason we don't allow ex-felons to vote?" Serena threw in another quarrel for discussion. "If you are out of prison, that means you have paid your debt to society and should be reinstated as a voter."

"You know that giving space for an authority to distribute voter ID cards is a way of policing the voting process, and policing works against people of color. So, that's a no!" Will Lee stated firmly.

"Even when it allows people of questionable character to vote?" Serena asked.

"Are you listening to yourself?" her father cried out. "Resident's registration office is where we start from nil; we get no Black people at the polls. You do know that the police are automatically against Black people, and that will further spur racism against us, right?"

"Okay, Serena, I kinda agree with Dad here. Resident's registration office will cause discrimination at polling polls," Jim affirmed.

"Thank you, Jim," Mr. Lee expressed his feelings for his son with his eyes.

"I understand. But that does not mean there aren't any ways we can ensure that suffrage IDs with photos are provided by the authority in advance," Serena declared.

"I understand you too, Serena, but only if it can be done appropriately," Mr. Lee said, hopefully.

~ ~ ~

There seems to be a lot of back and forth between William Lee and his children, especially Serena. This back and forth puts so much into perspective, and we get to listen, examine, and evaluate the challenges that surround voting in

America. We will also see how these challenges could be surmounted.

Objectively, Serena serves as the voice of the people against the system, which is represented by her father, who was a slave when he was a young man. She proffers so many logical answers and solutions to many of America's voting problems, and this highlights how we might be able to overcome the struggles with voting in America. All we need to have is the will to allow all citizens the right to cast their votes, just as the Founding Fathers imagined.

Conclusion

The struggle to get democracy right in America is real, and every effort made by each president—past or present—either exalts or undermines this struggle. Over time, there have been several attempts to define democracy in terms of what the leaders do rather than in terms of what the Constitution tells them to do.

Although these attempts may be seen by many as patriotic, they show that there are faults that hinder democracy itself. They need to be examined, no matter how patriotic they may seem. The argument stands that democracy should, without exception, be viewed from the people's perspective, and not from the perspective of the leaders alone and what they deem as right for the populace.

These phrases show you how democracy ought to work in allowing people to exercise their voting rights. True, the United States uses representative government like many other countries, but representative government still leaves room for the wishes of the majority over the minority. This is even more reason to ensure that the American people's right is not confined by additional rules set up by any leader.

The truth remains that voting is the most democratic action that allows the American people to have a say in their own governance. Hence, its integrity should be protected as much as possible. It doesn't help that the Electoral College may defeat the people's wishes at times, but the general election still goes a long way in representing the people's wishes, which is what these paragraphs are intended to highlight.

In his farewell address, George Washington warned darkly of the "baneful effects of the spirit of party generally."

Observations

The Founding Fathers meet again in 2021, in Washington, D.C. They sit around a fireplace sipping the modern version of their favored gin and discuss the actual situation of American politics.

"These last few weeks we have had an opportunity to look at today's political life. What did you gentlemen observe?" asked the first president of the United States.

"The political situation in the U.S. is dominated by partisan interest." Alexander Hamilton rose first, to oblige his leader. "I am surprised to see that party propaganda is all around. Politicians thirst for power and party supporters' dogmatism obscures the country's problems, which are often put off for years. I see topics like immigration, social legislation, infrastructure, taxes, and more," he reported.

John Adams took the next turn. "The hunger and selfishness of the politicians for re-election is so dominant that it often appears they are perpetually running for office and only filling in with the workings of the government when they have the time. First comes the ego, then the party ideology; the interest of the whole country plays a secondary role. I can hardly believe this behavior!" To John Adams, the behaviors he spoke of, which they had all witnessed, were near mutiny.

"Did you see how they handle special interests?" Thomas Jefferson asked. "They are actually writing individual interests and special requests right into laws. Taxes are the most popular topic to prove that. When individuals and interest groups campaign for tax breaks, this is quickly reflected in their own income or to the liquid assets.

Exceptions are mentioned that make sense for high incomes only and are ultimately not taxed. They are secured by the parliamentary process in such a way that their content often produces absurdities—and injustices. The richest American pays less taxes than his executives. These packaged special interests become mainstream simply through their application, and then they can no longer be challenged, as they are legally approved. This is a special way of harnessing legislation!" and he showed his disdain in his face.

"I imagine that there is a vicious cycle of feelings at play here," Washington commented. "First, a fear of losing dominance over 'people of color' and immigrants; after that, racial hatred, which is linked with white supremacism. That would be the basic pattern as I see it today."

"I do not agree with you at all, dear George," Jefferson answered back. "The country in the twenty-first century is divided into classes: the very rich, the rich, the middle class, and the poor. Rich, White people, mainly those on the right, care about maintaining and expanding their power and wealth."

Washington stated after a deep sigh: "Did you hear of the Rust Belt? It is a region from Illinois to western New York. That successful heavy industry has been in continuous decline since the 1980s. Factories closed their doors, laying off the workers, and to this day there have been no alternatives, no other industries that settled there nor provided income for the people. If you lose your job because factories stop their activities, you suffer the loss of livelihood. A personal disaster! In this case, what is your hope?"

Jefferson replied: "Many people support political slogans to get a solution. That might be a base for party loyalty."

"Well, White Americans feel like strangers in their home-towns," Hamilton pointed out. "It should be noted that their grandparents were immigrants themselves, and they changed the political and sociological situation at that time."

"Let us be honest," Jefferson interjected. "These are negative feelings that express insecurity in one's own soul. This feeling of insecurity carries over into the political process. Examples of this uncertainty are the many regulations restricting the voting process; for example, reducing the number of polling stations or restricting opening hours and more."

Washington asked the country's third president, "Tom, do you imagine it is an inferiority complex that leads to all the violence we've seen, not to mention the bossiness of so many people in charge of things? Anyone who thinks and acts differently becomes an enemy—"

"Yes—" Adams said, jumping out of his seat before Jefferson could reply, "and the enemy is also American—that's what makes for an absurdity! The situation pulls one party's politicians toward ideologically inflexible positions."

"I see that many Americans have the belief that their form of democracy is unique, correct, and superior. They don't see the partisan orientation of the political process as a problem. Many political leaders, and part of the national press, are likewise guided by uncivil discourse to maintain their ideological power," Jefferson uttered, half to himself, as if he were trying to wrap his thoughts around such a conversation.

And Hamilton added: "And it is also human to see that all creatures view those who are not like them as a threat and thus with disdain."

"Did you come across this?" asked Washington, of no one in particular. "Many Americans believe that democracy is a valued fact only when their own party is winning. That is poor understanding of civics and democratic rules, I admit. It seems that the lack of knowledge in civics and democratic rules has turned American politics to all that strong partisan thinking—don't you think this is true? It's very strange!"

"What I would like to mention," Hamilton interjected, "is this: Americans are raised to win—period! The rules of sport are dominating the political thinking, and that is wrong. In the politics of a democratic republic, different rules are important at different times. You must be ready to compromise for practical solutions."

"I can see this," Washington agreed. "The other party member is not an enemy but must be a partner. That is the context in which American politicians must work together. The partner is another American citizen, and that is what we worked so hard to put in place for them. Yes, they ought to be all for one and one for all, even though some will lose office and others will win it. It's not the victory of the candidate—it's the victory of the country that matters. How can a country survive without compromises?"

Adams quite agreed with his old friend. "You are wholly correct on that," he told Washington. "The opponents of the American parties are not the other parties, but abroad, probably in China and Russia, both of which strive for global dominance and to limit or diminish the influence of the USA. American politics and American politicians—and the party ideologues—should be concerned with this threat and not with the absolute dominance of one American over the other. I really wonder about this lack of analysis!"

"And to be honest," brooded Jefferson, "the actual bipartisan competition is polarized not only by the partisan ideologies but caused and boosted by the media and tech companies, which act in the name of profit only. They should all be blamed. Many times, the parties support or favor extreme views in order to attract primary voters, who tend to be on the extreme end of their party. Then you have the online news sites and the social media sites like Facebook. They first get to know your political affiliation and then they send you stories about the 'crazies' in the other party to get you to click on those articles. So, conservatives start to think the liberals are all looney, and vice versa."

At that, the Founding Fathers rose and grumbled among themselves on this great matter. All agreed that the parties themselves had gone too far away from what they had intended.

"The fight in everyday political life is very often a critical view of the other party member— 'the other Americans,'" said Hamilton, expressing what they were all feeling. "I picked up anonymous denunciations, blackmailing, denigrating, denouncing mistakes, naming weak points, criticizing with the harshest mockery—these are the common ways to defeat the 'other.' What is missing is a positive claim, recognizing similarities, and building solutions on them."

Jefferson took the floor to say, "I recently remarked on a new/old trick in American politics: voter restrictions. Yes, voter restrictions! We, back in the seventeenth century, were trapped in our notion that the ideal voter could take up arms to defend the country. So, yes, we did not think to include women, slaves, and non-landowners in the vote with that in mind. The last two hundred years have brought about a rethinking of that in many aspects. The enlarged voter base is truly in favor of democratic thinking; it has grown into that. These limitations of restricted voting hours and fewer ballot boxes, and further formal regulations, are clearly a step backward."[1]

"I believe that the question of race is still the great unresolved problem of American society," Hamilton added, sadly. "It was an unsolved problem for us at the time, and it still is."

"And to be honest," Washington, too, sadly brought up that "the U.S. has lost its role-model status as the leading democracy in the world. They can no longer claim the leadership for the West since moral values and virtues are hardly fulfilled anymore. The American internal quarrels are well-registered in the world. For many outsiders of the U.S. who thought so highly of the American experience, it is a sad day!"

"Looking back in 2020, and even further, to 2016, is frightening. Those were not ordinary races, and the Republican candidate was not an ordinary candidate." Adams was speaking now. "Many Republicans latched on to the saying that, whereas Trump's critics took him literally but not seriously, his supporters took him seriously but not literally."[2]

---

[1] "Of the eleven states with the highest Black turnout in 2008, seven adopted stricter voter ID laws. Of the twelve states that experienced the highest rates of Hispanic population growth in 2000 and 2010, nine passed laws making it harder to vote. " Levitsky/Ziblatt, *How Democracies Die* (New York, 2019), p. 185.
[2] Levitsky/Ziblatt, p. 60

"It seems to me that a minority is only successful when they're using silly tricks, like Eldridge Gerry's redrawing the voting map and introducing peculiar electoral laws to satisfy the political majority. The voters themselves are just being shuttled around to where the politicians move them, like on a chessboard."

"What is the saying: If you can't win the game, change the rules...."

"Exactly!" the Fathers all chimed in.

Adams had more to say. "Here's another strange fact I've noticed: Christians are acting against Christianity nowadays. Basic Christian values are disregarded by the right-wing Evangelicals. As I understand it, charity should be the driving force behind social justice. Instead, as Christians, they get involved in the political circus and cannot even endorse mandatory health care, which is solidarity work. There is also something they call the 'Tea Party,' whose members all think just alike. I do not understand it at all!"

"In the bigger context," Hamilton chimed in, "I must ask, is fascism or authoritarianism at the door?"

"I agree with what you are implying, Alex," Washington told his colleague. "The partisan division has taken on bizarre features in the country. The opponent of an American is seen in the other party rather than abroad, for example, in Russia or China. We spoke of this before, but it is very true. I cannot follow this argument. Surely the country will weaken in this position, and maybe even become vulnerable to outsiders.

"The willingness to use physical force to enforce one's own preferences increased significantly in 2020. They say they have something they call 'polling', that has uncovered *this* information: up to 15 percent of Americans are generally willing to use violence as a political weapon. To be honest, we had violent times back then. But we should have learned something meanwhile. They say that this proportion is more pronounced among Republicans than among Democrats. Amazing!"

"Well, I'm glad we all agree," Jefferson remarked. "Physical violence as an expression of political enforcement *is* the beginning of fascism. At least it is anti-democratic. Violence is a key factor in fascism. I never even thought about whether this development could take root in our country or not. We were happy just to get independence from Great Britain so we could carry out our intentions to build democratic rules for our growing republic."

"Fascism is a form of far-right, authoritarian, ultranationalism characterized by dictatorial power, isn't that right?" Hamilton asked. "Yes," Jefferson nodded, "with forcible suppression of the opposition, and strong regimentation of society and of the economy, which came to prominence in early twentieth-century Europe in Germany, in Italy, and in the Soviet Union, today Russia. Is this an upcoming danger for the U.S.?"

"To be honest, it could be a political philosophy, a movement, or a regime that exalts a nation, and often race, above the individual," Washington explained, "and that stands for a centralized autocratic government headed by a dictatorial leader, severe economic and social regimentation, and forcible suppression of opposition. I never thought this would be an American problem, but things could move in that direction if our problems and our anger continue to escalate

"I am so concerned about the political situation here in 2020," he went on. "We intended to break deliberately the power of governing, to prevent the federal government from being able to govern alone. Fundamental rights, the rule of law, popular rule, separation of powers, independent jurisdiction, the right to oppose: these values must be deeply rooted in the country."

Washington frowned and mused: "All of a sudden, the belief in the government is absolute. What I see nowadays is a very skeptical view toward the power in Washington D.C. Americans have an ambivalent attitude toward their country; they are very suspicious. Whatever is proposed is criticized by somebody. And now, these people are longing for a fundamental change—a strong political figure would solve all problems. I cannot understand this hope."

"What is needed is broad support of democratic rules. That means that every American can make his political decisions based on ethics and values and that the result is respected," Jefferson reasoned. "To follow enthusiastically big names is not a goal or a solution."

Hearing this conversation, Adams jumped up and shrieked, "Did we mention the riot on January 6, 2021? My God, poor America!"

January 7, 2021

The Constitution of America was formed through sleepless nights of discussions and debates among the Founding Fathers. But as noteworthy as these efforts were, the Constitution is not without its faults. Perhaps the defense might be that the Founding Fathers did not envisage America becoming a leading nation in the world, one that would need a more comprehensive constitution with spelled-out conditions and clauses. Nevertheless, that was 230 years ago, and now, America might be reeling from the effect of these shortcomings.

When we fast-forward to present-day America, where the people once again in the nation's history struggle to believe in their democratic systems and institutions and are quick to call "foul," we should not hastily say they are just being "people." There might be some elements of truth in the fact that the American system—the electoral system, for one—is not entirely perfect in determining a world leader.

~ ~ ~

The four Fathers met again on January 7, 2021, in the Old Ebbitt Grill in Washington—one day after the storming of the U.S. Capitol.

"Did you see the events of yesterday?" asked John Adams. "The storming of the Capitol was televised! Wow, it's amazing how quickly the news is being shared these days."

"I am still shocked by the pictures of the storming of the House of Congress on Capitol Hill," Thomas Jefferson bemoaned. "I just can't believe how you can do something like that. This building is the epitome of American democracy!"

"I am shocked, too," George Washington added. "Broken windows, smashed doors, people in strange robes and headgear. Some had hard objects in their hands and looked menacing. There were flags of all kinds. It was just like the riots we saw in our days."

"I too was appalled by these invaders," Alexander Hamilton sadly spoke. "What was the reason for this? I did not get that. Why this turmoil?"

"The focal point was the final act in electing the new president," Washington spoke directly to Hamilton. "The counting of the electoral votes was certified by The Congress. With that, the new president was declared elected and confirmed. Still, the defeated president tried to turn the results to his favor without any reason or evidence to support his claim that he had won the election. That *that* would be as a presumption…simply unbelievable! It was our intention, after all, to elect people from the people based on democratic principles. Automatic re-election is a step back to monarchy-like governance …where the successor is chosen by a closed circle of men, not by 'the people.'"

"That can only mean that democratic action is not accepted by many," Hamilton nearly cried out. "I am surprised to state the truth of it: Some Americans are not democracy-minded!"

"Looking at this day in that perspective gives us an unprecedented act of civic disorder," Washington added. "What's going on in this country? What would be an effective remedy to this situation?"

"I should consider a better knowledge of civics is needed," Adams pronounced. "Our beloved Americans have to learn more about governing a republic. Democratic rules are essential!"

Partisan Politics

Now, in 2021, the group of Founding Fathers sit together in Washington, D.C. in Blair House. This time their aim is to discuss the striking animosity between the American political parties. They will reflect on the reasons as well as search the nation's history to get an idea of the situation. As the leader, George Washington begins the exploration.

~ ~ ~

"Gentlemen, I see the two American parties today ideologically purer than they were before the turn of the millennium. Their profiles are clear. The conservative democrats and the liberal republicans who found solutions in the twentieth century are gone. The parties are addressing a clearly defined profile that they offer to the constituency. Let us begin our dialog there."

Thomas Jefferson spoke first. "Every American citizen should and *must* choose the values propagated by these parties. As there are only two profiles, it must be easy to take the measure of the values someone can stand for."

Alexander Hamilton saw the matter from another angle. "In my view, with the Democratic Party, social problems and contexts are recognized and linked to possible solutions. The welfare state is to be expanded to enable every American to lead a dignified life. That is brave and, in fact, it is a huge commitment."

"Their intention is that government regulations and tax revenues should fund the solutions," John Adams chimed in.

Hamilton continued. "I like to see that this party's profile is a rainbow coalition. Many opinions are brought together."

"And this party favors civil rights," Adams responded. "That is a big difference from our times, and that is new for me. Officially, we only thought of the upper class of the residents at that time. Let's be honest, for us there were no female voters, and certainly no natives and slaves."

"True," Hamilton agreed. "The government should recognize the interests of the community and strive for minimum solutions for the good of all. Many worries and problems can only be solved in community. In fact, the government has a positive role to play."

"I read about a political slogan that suggested government is not the solution but the problem," Jefferson blurted out. "I'm speechless! What does this mean? It was our sincere intention, after all, to form a new state, different from the British Kingdom, and aspiring to a new kind of society run by capable people *from among the common people.* Right?"

Washington answered. "I agree fully with that statement." It was silent for a moment.

"Government activity is probably addressed here," Washington continued. "It must be efficient and not waste the tax revenues of the citizens."

Now, it was Hamilton agreeing. "This is a clear and good request. I can fully agree with it. It is a simple principle, understandable for everyone, and it can well fulfill our ideal image from back then."

"In recent decades, the federal government has been spending much more than it takes in. The amounts are huge...," Jefferson brought into the discussion. "Not many people believe this is the right approach to fixing America's problems...unless we could figure out a way for the super-rich to contribute much more."

"That is very true," Hamilton admitted.

"The other party has remained culturally and politically homogeneous," Adams offered. "White Protestant voters express their concerns: the liberal credo with low profile of government, low taxes, high personal freedom, few government activities. It is the party of the racial status quo."

"Looking back to the last century," Washington began, "I see two internally heterogeneous parties. As they were polarized within their members, they could find compromises over the boundaries and were able to build a reasonable politics in many details."

"The different governments, regardless of the party color, mastered many differences," Jefferson pointed out, "like the Great Depression in the 1930s, the Cold War after 1945, the move toward more social legislation. The second half of the twentieth century was the time of the Pax Americana, the worldwide dominance of American leadership."

"American values of the free-market economy and democratic rules to govern were widespread all over the world. That was a good time," added Hamilton.

"President Johnson's Civil Rights and Voting Rights Acts prompted a massive shift in party identification," Washington reminded them. "Both parties became internally more homogeneous—it was the end of the partisan cooperation. It democratized the South by authorizing mainly Black voters to have full citizens' rights."

"Still, today," Adams explained, "one party is the primary representative of minority and first- and second-generation immigrant voters, while voters of the other party remain overwhelmingly White."

"I see a split along party lines in the political landscape. The party ideologies are very strong. Political commonalities are rarely sought. The defamation of the other party is widespread and apparently very successful in the election campaigns," Jefferson stated.

"For my understanding I cannot see how this should work," he continued. "In our time, the effort was great to find new ways. We didn't agree on many details, but our intention was to forge a new homeland, America.

"In fact," he continued, "the clear party profiles in ideology are catastrophic for this country. The political process is dysfunctional, or I would even say 'rigged.' That is confrontational behavior. The party bosses look for differences and blow them up into a fundamental opposition."

"In this climate of distrust and aggressive attacks," Hamilton explained, "a democracy is not able to act. Possible solutions are examined in the party discipline. Any compromise is presented and understood as defeat.

"And I must add," he rose to the occasion, "it is seen as an admission of weakness. That is so strange!"

"I remember the slogan: The party is always right—the dreaded principle of the communist parties in the former Soviet Union, what today is Russia, and China. That is the reality lived in the USA today," Adams concluded, clasping his hands over his prominent belly, and then started again. "Belief in the party's ideology is growing stronger and stronger, along with distrust of the other party."

"I think we spoke of this at our last meeting," Washington said. "The other party is considered to be the real enemy of the country, while a real enemy is from the outside. That is so strange to me. The enemy of the U.S. is someone whose intention is to destroy the political structure of our Constitution."

Hamilton jumped to his feet. "I agree that it is someone outside of our boundary. But to be honest, the intention of an authoritarian might have the same effect. Mistrust of our institutions, and an intention to override democratic rules."

"That is poison for a democracy," Adams declared firmly. "It might be the first step toward authoritarianism. The political participants want to be right. Only their own proposed solution should apply.

"Politics nowadays do not look for a compromise; a third way as a way out in a confrontation is not considered. Yet, my friends, compromising is precisely the high art of democratic behavior."

Nodding in agreement, Jefferson picked up Adams's point. "Until recently, religious beliefs, the culture of your home, your own skin color, or your gender were the indications that you had found your political family—to have the idea of the desired political values."

"Yet," Adams responded, "the personal decision to vote for a party was based on information. What you read in the newspapers, magazines, and books, as well as discussions in the family and with your friends—these things were essential."

"It seems to me," Hamilton started, "that this behavior has changed, or reversed to the prime information of the statements of party ideology. People express their attachment to their party first. As a prime orientation, today they repeatedly take the party ideology that they have already chosen for themselves. They adopt the values and statements of the print media and electronic sources, which are already heavily ideologized."

"Again," Adams enunciated his position. "This seems to me to be the reaction of a good party communist. *Yes, the party is always right'* is very dangerous!

"The U.S. still has no political culture with recognized democratic rules!"

"No wonder," Jefferson agreed, "since civics has not been a school subject for many years."

Washington chimed in, "That is a big lack in the country's education system and should be changed immediately.

"There was a Representative in the 1990s who used these words: 'You are fighting a war, a war for more power to build a party majority.' I was frightened to read this statement. We were not at war during our discussions in Philadelphia, yet we worked on a common goal. We had a war with Great Britain, but within the community of politicians, we did not agree on many details and fought for our points of view, but we respected each other's meaning."

"I am with you, Mr. President," Hamilton assured Washington, "that seems to be the politics of warfare in the 1990s. I believe it was called the 'Republican Revolution'. It was, or still is, nasty.

"They go so far to attack the opponent that they lack patriotism, and they are, in fact, not acting as Americans. That is nonsense, pure nonsense. We are all Americans, and we should stand together and find common ground to fix problems."

Jefferson reminded the Founding Fathers: "Since we arrived in 2020, there are many states—I heard forty-eight states out of fifty—that intend to re-invent voter restrictions. That is the behavior of the 1870s, which was known in the southern states as Jim Crow legislation. After the Civil War, which gave the slaves full rights to go on ballots, their power to have a vote was indirectly thwarted, or evaded, by voting restrictions that made it harder for mostly low-income minority citizens to go to vote. That is not democratic. That is a kind of authoritarianism."

"I would see this behavior as supremacist," Hamilton spoke sadly, "as it is against the Black people. Awful!"

"All details of voter restrictions help to legitimate the use of uncivil discourse! Yes, that is a support of undemocratic behavior," Adams said definitively, then continued:

"There is one proposition for the voting process I can admit, and that is the voting card with photograph to authorize the citizens to participate on the ballot. That might be invented, as there are no resident registration offices in the country. In Europe, the voter documents are delivered by the local authorities to your officially registered address by mail."

"Friends," Washington began to speak as he stood up, "did you hear about the mantra-like mention of voter fraud, now, for years? This is ridiculous. And our American authorities should not be able to conduct the elections? I cannot believe this claim."

"Oh my God!" Adams yelled. "Have we really fallen to that level?"

"If the voting process is not fully established for all Americans," Hamilton threatened, "the country is not fully democratized after 230 years of existence!

"Let us hope that democratic rules are more seriously respected!"

The Ethics of Democracy

"Governing a country is not a sports event with a winning and a losing team, but a process of compromising to make the entire population the winner."

—Werner Neff, *Restore Our Democracy*

It is an art to govern democratically, to have the experience of using democratic rules and ethical values, and to have civilized and correct governing. Democracy has been set to operate in a way that establishes fair governing through the leaders to the led. A functioning democracy knows rules are important for the political decision-making process. So, while it is true that democracy operates with rules, these rules are to be trusted and abided by the people who lead the nation.

Democracy originates from the Greek word *demokratia,* which means "rule of the people," which was derived from *demos*, "people," and *kratos*, "power" or "rule," in the fifth century B.C. By implication, "rule of the people" means that the people govern through a particular individual or a set of particular individuals who they have trusted enough to represent their interests equally.

Yet, the ever-inquisitive Lenard, George Washington's curious nephew, has evaluated twenty-first century democracy and thinks that it is just a parody of the real thing. Now, he doesn't just conclude that we do not practice democracy; he thinks we have modified it to suit the interest of the leaders we do not really want, but who may be our best shot at governing.

∼∼∼

"But how is democracy selecting just one single person to rule millions of people?" Lenard asks. He genuinely wants to know.

"Well, I mean, he is not there to represent his own interests," his Uncle George cited. "He is there for the people, to represent their wishes. Besides, that's a vision-shortening way of viewing things. Too much attention is paid to me, George Washington, as the leader of a nation in 1791, while there is little, or no attention paid to the other leaders."

"The other leaders?" Lenard asked sarcastically.

"The governors, mayors, etc. That's why it is called a democracy. If only one person were to rule, then that's an autocracy—not a democracy," Washington explained.

"That's just division of labor—not division of powers. The governors and mayors are still subject to Washington. It is no different from an autocratic rule where the ruler has people who work for him," Lenard pointed out.

"Oh my God," Washington listened and laughed, "there is no end to your reasoning. You see, Lenard, I like the part where you call it 'division of labor' rather than division of powers. Sometimes, it works like that in America, but it is not all the time. There is a difference."

"What difference, Uncle?" Lenard asked, slightly afraid of being disproved.

"In an autocratic government, the only thing that works, as you pointed out, is division of labor—not power. This means the leader cannot be checked, and he reigns sovereign. His decisions are final and cannot be revoked. Compare that to a republic with democratic rules, I didn't reign supreme. My decisions were subject to the other governing bodies, like the legislature and the judiciary. I can be called to order, and Lenard, if I'm found guilty of misconduct or misdemeanor, I can be impeached."

"Impeached?" Lenard asked with sudden realization.

"Lenard, I know America is all about the country first. But what a lot of people don't understand is that the people *are* the country. Without the people, there is no America. So, when we mean that we are acting in the best interest of the country, we mean we are acting in the best interest of *America*."

"Yes, but the funny thing about America's democracy is how we say we are all about freedom but still find a way to justify the injustice done against African Americans."

Washington sighed. "The truth is that, if we had intended that slavery should continue in America, African Americans would not have gained their freedom so long ago," Washington bemoaned.

"See? That's my point! Intention. Honestly, I feel like African Americans becoming free was more of a plan rather than an admission of wrongdoing. Uncle, Americans traded slaves for over 250 years! The only reason they decided to set African Americans free was because they felt America was beginning to become a model country and slavery was not a good look on their impending status."

"Okay, Lenard, I think…"

"In February 2020," Lenard started, interrupting his uncle, "a young Black man jogging in his hometown in Georgia was shot in the street by two White men while they were driving their truck. They said they believed they were pursuing an intruder in their neighborhood. The two pursuers were father and son, a retired police officer and a sporting goods store owner. When a dispute arose between the jogger, who was unarmed, and the pursuers, they killed him on the spot. Later they were convicted."

Washington was stopped in his tracks by that remark of his nephew. All he could say was, "That's very sad."

"Exactly! So, I understand that democracy is all about equality and individual freedom but let us not assume that some people don't get a pass because of their status, or the color of their skin. Democracy may be about fairness, but the way the world has been reshaped by people, it's become naturally unfair. It's like everyone is living in this pretend world."

"I honestly don't know what to say. I mean, do I think that everything you have told us is true, yes. But as much as I agree with you, I want you to know that democracy has never been shaped to work in that way," Washington was firm in his position.

"Really?" Lenard asked.

"Yes. And there must be a place in your heart where you believe in the power of democracy in America, and hope people abide by its fair principles."

"But how long do we continue to hope, Uncle, when the obvious stares us in the face?" Lenard asked, with concern in his voice.

The first president stood up and held Lenard's hands in his own. "As humans, that's all we can do, my dear boy. I wish I had a better answer for you."

~ ~ ~

For the first time, Lenard may be right, not only about the democracy in America but about twenty-first century democracy. We all know the rules that guide democracy—but it appears that these rules are not all followed to the letter, because we have come up with our own version of what we think a democratic society should look like.

Conclusion

The American Constitution is not precise in many details. There are some subjects the Constitution does not address at all. Therefore, the question becomes: How do we know what exactly the other unspoken parts are saying?

Once again, through dialog, we see George Washington trying to explain these theoretical and unspoken parts of the Constitution to his nephew, Lenard, on the part of the interpretation of the Constitution, and how the document has been "unanimously" agreed upon by the citizens of America. Apparently, even he is at a loss concerning the gaps in America's written Constitution. Nevertheless, before we hastily conclude that America's written Constitution is faulty, we must search for an objective point of view about its truths.

There have been so many things to juggle at the same time when it comes to the role of American partisan politics in America's political problems. We must examine whether or not American partisan politics plays a significant role in America's political problems, and whether this role is the consequence of the Founding Fathers' actions.

It's all about examining the truths of American political history!

What Are Democratic Rules?

- Every democratic act is characterized by respect, benevolence, and fairness.
- Every contribution in a democratic discussion is received with understanding.
- Any suggestions are treated orderly and with respect.
- If you do not agree with an idea, you agree not to agree.
- All participants have equal rights.
- There is a hierarchy of laws.
- The ruling of a republic is based on free and fair elections.
- The higher the voter turnout, the higher the justification of the politicians.
- The elections must include all entitled and interested parties. The organization must be open and fair.
- The majority of votes determines the political course.
- Political discussion must be conducted with decency and respect, by all from all.

2040

A Look Back

John Miller, the forty-ninth president of the United States, has invited the Founding Fathers to the White House in Washington, D.C. Let's listen in on their conversation:

President Miller opened the door to the Oval Office, and began with: "Gentlemen, welcome to the White House! It is probably the first time you have entered this great House. Please feel comfortable."

The small group of Founding Fathers hesitated when entering, looked around and were led to seats.

"Dear Mr. President, thank you for inviting us to your official residence," George Washington spoke for the group. "I must admit, it is a nice home here in the center of Washington. Can you enjoy these lofty surroundings with all your tasks?"

Once all the gentlemen were seated comfortably in their chairs, the President spoke.

"I have no problem so far," John Miller replied. "The political situation has calmed down a lot in recent years, as there have been some important changes. You know, I am elected now for six years. It allows me to focus on politics and therefore on political solutions. There is time to seek and find political majorities. Re-election is out of the question."

Thomas Jefferson stood up. "We see other changes that are reducing the excesses of recent decades," he told the President honestly. "Life elections for Supreme Court justices have been reduced to twenty years—that still is a long period to be on the job. We intended to guarantee the justices' independence absolute."

"It is true that the independence of the judiciary concerned us greatly," John Adams spoke for the Fathers, who showed their agreement by nodding their heads. "We assumed that there was a neutral stance there on political issues, but that is very conceptual.

"In our time, this notion was certainly permissible. We wanted to free ourselves from British rule through the royal house and take on new political responsibilities," Adams explained.

Alexander Hamilton added, "The structure of state power should be clearly divided into three units. This was the idea first developed by Aristotle, the fourth century B.C. Greek, as well as later by the Enlightener, John Locke, from England, and the Frenchman, Montesquieu. We dealt intensively with the writings of these thinkers."

James Madison chimed in with, "We had to fill the three levels of state authority with these ideas, even invent them. We were the first to dare to abandon the feudal order and build something new."

"The structure of government in Britain was, and still is today, in 2040, centered on the royal family," Washington reminded his colleagues. "Successors were and still are chosen from within the royal family. Often, the most suitable person from the family is not chosen, but it is the first-born principle that is chosen." He stood, slightly angered, and added, with a wave of his pointer finger, "That is, in fact, absurd!"

Adams picked it up from there. "It's now 250 years since the country has been governed with republican principles and democratic rules. We feel this as an amazing feat...just great. Not everything was brilliant, but the principles have been adopted by other states as a good basis." Everyone in the group seemed to agree.

"What has been known for many years," Washington pointed out, "is that what is needed is not only a good constitutional text, but also ethical and properly democratic behavior on the part of the members of Congress.

"We must truly admit that our intention was to establish a good Constitution, not more. In fact, in my presidency, I set some unwritten rules for our young country, and the new style of government served as a good example of responsible behavior. Today, we can name some of these unwritten rules that we felt would be essential for good political governing.

"Mutual respect, mutual tolerance, and the sincere understanding of others are the keys to a successful government–that still applies! Let it summarize as civic virtues.

"We saw so many books that underline these aspects, some of which we read recently, as well. I am impressed by how many people are now involved in politics in a way of good governing."

President Miller responded, "Yes, the last few years do show that. We were able to resolve the tense situation from the turn of the century well into the 2020s. We no longer regard the other party member as a dead-end enemy. The splitting of the two major parties from back then into four smaller parties allows for compromises to be possible, since three of the new parties can decide something, and they can do so with respectable majorities.

"For one thing, the fighting mood that arose in the 1990s has waned. Politics is seen today as a process of understanding, of finding the problems—even anticipating them. The split between the two major parties has contributed to substantive solutions being sought."

Miller looked around and continued. "What is new is that the deputies in the Senate and the House of Representatives have limited terms of twelve years each. Senators can be re-elected once; House members five times.

"The prescribed terms of office allow time to be spent searching for good solutions. That's been a great feature.

"During the past Congress periods, some issues have been addressed. When it came to immigration, agreement was reached on a new residence statute. The red card allows foreign workers to come to the U.S. for a limited time, and then they legally leave the country after six months and come back the next year. I wouldn't think that would work out, nor would the democrats support it—too much to-ing and fro-ing for school kids and jobs." Miller stopped a moment and cleared his throat.

"Tensions at the border have decreased significantly. People have been traveling in and out legally since 2036.

"The truth is, we need these workers for seasonal work, mainly in agriculture. It seems a good solution for both sides: us, the country, with fluctuating workload, and them, the workers. They must be happy to ensure the livelihood of their families and earning a good income compared to their local possibilities. It is true that they leave their hometown and are far from their families and their culture some of the time, though."

Madison raised the question that was on the minds of the Founding Fathers. "Do you remember the strange moments on the southern border, when we were here on our last visit in 2020, with the many trespassers who crossed the border illegally and thus became 'illegals'?"

Miller responded. "The situation is much better than it was then. Our country, and the States, now know who is coming. With the visa applications filed in our consulates abroad, we know them better. We have an overview of immigration, and since these people enter legally, they can also leave and come back legally.

"This solution was only possible through a collaboration of three parties and the support of various interest groups. All these interest groups used democratic norms and rules; they built a pro-democratic coalition. The goal was clear: to find a solution that promised mutual benefits and calmed the borders," President Miller admitted, and then continued.

"It was the first time in many years that a coalition of different political groups found a practical solution. The approval was great, both in Congress and in the affected districts. The inhabitants of the border strip had to bear a heavy burden for many years.

"The focus of the efforts was the will and the intention to find a good solution for our country, and for those most affected—the border residents and the workers."

Everyone nodded and paused for a thoughtful moment.

"Building up coalitions is difficult," Hamilton opined. "It is a political state-of-the-art process. It must have been most effective to bring together opposing political views in many details, but to have found a common base to agree on one problem at a time.... In our time, that would have been an act of defending American democracy itself. State legislators, different religious leaders, business leaders, and political activists finding common ground. Perfect. I love this kind of political process!"

Miller nodded his appreciation for the compliment, then continued with, "Three of the new parties were able to build a group to promote democratic rules—that was amazing!

That included conservative ideas and liberal wishes, which seemed at first impossible—but the love to keep our old democracy functioning was stronger!

"One party wanted to exclude the extreme positions in order to revive the once-successful center-right base. Then there was the split. The extreme groups included Christians, tax minimizers, gun enthusiasts, and outspoken white supremacists.

"One of the new, smaller parties now lives with clear conservative values. It welcomes—as in the past—a healthy financial policy with moderate taxes, and supports private initiative and personal responsibility, as well as long-term ethics. It's a wonderful new situation for the country!"

John Jay reflected, "That is a revival compared to the one in post-war Germany or Chile after a dictatorship."

Miller again nodded his appreciation before resuming. "In principle, there will be two schools of thought: the conservative, which upholds *old* values, and the liberal, which seeks changes and improvements. Both directions are to be recognized. Period. Political developments are wave movements between these two poles.

"The other party split because its desired goals were significantly different. Efforts had to be made to warm the working class to progressive ideas. One had to admit clearly that the income situation of many workers had stagnated for decades, and purchasing power was declining, while doubts about new prospects were spreading."

Benjamin Franklin spoke, looking thoughtful. "The commitment to higher wages, moderate working hours, and job security certainly appears to have paid off. Those who work should have a fair share of the result. I am pleased to find that this has been enforced somewhat more clearly in recent years."

"In our time," Jefferson brought up, "health insurance was unknown. What a good idea to replace possible future expenses with monthly contributions. I'm quite impressed about everything that has been invented in the meantime. Congratulations, President Miller, very nicely done."

Again, the group showed agreement with nods of their heads.

"Another good invention are the mandatory pension funds," Franklin added. "Campaigning for this must have been a big success for this party."

President Miller responded with, "Yes. Now, let's have a short break. I invite you for a glass of wine. Yes, wine. Back then you had gin.... The wine is today a more popular drink, especially in the evening. So let us toast to our country and its turn to the better!"

The men stood up and reached for their glasses. They toasted one another and their great efforts.

"I'd like to come back to the challenges of the deputies," Washington requested. "The ability of the deputies lies precisely in tracking down factual solutions to a problem and finding ways to compromise with others.

"The thinking and the ideas of the other party members must have been understood by all deputies; that is, they must have had the ability to take this different opinion as an expression of their will. You don't have to agree with that, but you have to acknowledge the other opinion."

"We saw, in 2020 and before," Jay piped up, "that there was a time when a party was fundamentally opposed to compromise. Only their own opinion was authoritative, and they would only allow their suggestions to be included in the laws. Doing politics in that way was close to monarchy; for example, the British king who had an opinion and wanted to enforce it. This was not the spirit of a republic that must follow democratic rules."

Hamilton agreed. "Forbearance and understanding make a constitution viable."

Washington spoke next, for the Fathers. "Respect for those who disagree, tolerance, and forbearance are unwritten rules in political life. This should apply to all democratically governed countries in the world. We feared that these important character traits had been severely weakened in the U.S. over the past few decades. I speak for all of us when I say we are grateful to discover they have been back for a few years, now."

"I hope forever," Adams stated loudly and firmly. Washington replied, "I agree!"

"Human behavior is part of ethics," Jefferson said. "It is a basic attitude that is not only important in politics, but every coexistence is based on ethical principles. Ethics is probably the most important quality of humanity."

Pointing to a copy of the Constitution that was framed and hung on the wall, Washington reminded his colleagues that: "The constitution as a set of rules in black and white is one side of the coin; human character traits is the other. This combination must be considered for the functioning of governance. The difficult side is educating man about ethics and values.

"Human behavior, character, ethical attitude: these are all educational characteristics that have to be worked out in the family, in the social environment, in school, and in religion!"

"Did you remember," Miller asked, once they were settled in with their wine glasses and enjoying the company, "that, in the 2020s, the U.S. was named to have the same democratic standards as Thailand and Turkey, as Venezuela and Colombia, or as Poland and Hungary? Just amazing. Our ranking is better now, at least for some steps.

"You can say the period from 1970 to 2024 was a democratic recession."

Washington, holding up his glass once again, articulated what they were all feeling, "The history of the U.S. shows ups and downs in this regard. Times of tension give way to calmer periods. I'm glad we're on a high this time, for the last time we were here was quite disheartening. I salute you, Mr. President."

"I have a question," Hamilton interrupted. "The countless voting restrictions we saw taking root twenty and more years ago, what became of them?"

"They have been lifted for the most part," President Miller was pleased to announce to the Founding Fathers. "The turnout on presidential elections has increased about 10 percent. Not bad!"

"It was a good process to have the electoral authorities in forty-one states changed the electoral laws for the better," Miller told them. "That meant for opening access and not restrictions here and there. The people feel addressed to select their representatives in Congress with a high turnout.

"It was also important that election day was moved to a weekend. The opening time of thirty-six hours from Saturday morning to Sunday evening is convenient and practical for many eligible voters.

"The introduction of a resident's registration office throughout the country also made it possible to send all eligible voters electronic voting cards. The cleanup of the electoral lists was complicated, though. It sometimes invited undemocratic measures, which were detrimental to voter turnout."

"Wow!" Madison shouted. "May I say this for all of us? We are happy that during the last two decades there have been small changes that have corrected the political situation of our country for the better. This is really marvelous!"

"Cheers!" Everyone was delighted!

Epilogue

Today, American history appears to be diluted by many irregularities. This book was written in a bid to confront and suggest how these irregularities might be corrected. As you have journeyed through these pages, the key incidents and events that highlighted the constitutional history of America were brought directly to you, the people.

The use of dialogs in this book should aid a better understanding of the events that led to the continual amendments of the Bill of Rights. As you have read, the discussions of the Founding Fathers led to so many realizations of the shortcomings of "The Bill," as well as spoken of the need for certain remedies.

You have also been presented with the importance of some actions that were taken to protect the autonomy of America in its early life. Many people have always viewed the concession of the Founding Fathers at the Second Continental Congress as an unnecessary one, that made Britain extend its neo-colonialist rule on America for a longer period. In this book, the analysis shows how this concession was the single factor that set America on a journey of gradual autonomy.

Most of the changes we see in America today contribute to the hard truths that accompanied the discussions of the Founding Fathers. For example, Alexander Hamilton's insistence on the disparity between equal rights given to some and not other groups of people led to conscious efforts to include women in administrative and governmental affairs, and free Black people, albeit after 250 years of slavery.

The facts remain that the Founding Fathers laid the foundation for the development of America, and what we call "The Land of Dreams" today, was not forged out of perfect automatic decisions from very wise people. True, the Founding Fathers were wise and strategic, but wise and strategic people make mistakes, too. These mistakes made it possible to correct the ideology of having a confederation for young America.

Symbolically, the discussions of the Founding Fathers represent the way everyone should sit with others to examine their decisions to make America better.

This book significantly presents the actions of the Founders as a reminder that every decision you make to improve America—no matter how little they may seem—makes you a Founding Father, or Mother, for the next generations to come.

Dear Reader,

Have you met the Founding Fathers lately?

Bibliography

Dorsey Armstrong
Years that Changed History: 1215
The Teaching Company, Chantilly, VA, 2019

Richard Bell
Ordinary Americans in the Revolution
The Teaching Company, Chantilly, VA, 2021

Aaron Blake
"Why are there only two parties in American politics?" [2016], Accessed on 2/18/2022 https://www.washingtonpost.com/news/the-fix/wp/2016/04/27/why-are-there-only-two-parties-in-american-politics/

William R. Cook
Tocqueville and the American Experiment
The Teaching Company, Chantilly, VA, 2004

Encyclopaedia Britannica
The Founding Fathers
The Essential Guide to The Men Who Made America
John Wiley & Sons, Inc., Hoboken, NJ

J. Rufus Fears
A History of Freedom
The Teaching Company, Chantilly, VA, 2001

J. Rufus Fears
The Wisdom of History
The Teaching Company, Chantilly, VA, 2007

Winston Groom
The Patriots
Alexander Hamilton, Thomas Jefferson, John Adams, and the Making of America
National Geographic Partners, LLD, Washington DC, 2020

Allen C. Guelzo
The American Mind
The Teaching Company, Chantilly, VA, 2005

Allen C. Guelzo
America's Founding Fathers,
The Teaching Company, Chantilly, VA, 2017

Jacob S. Hacker and Paul Person
American Amnesia, How the War on Government Led Us to Forget What Made America Prosper
Simon & Schuster, New York, 2016

William G. Hurst
Our Great Political Divide, Causes, Impacts, and Prospects
Baroda, Michigan, 2021

Sean Illing,
"How do we know if we're in a constitutional crisis? 11 experts explain." Vox, May 16, 2019, Accessed on 2/23/2022
https://www.vox.com/2019/5/16/18617661/donald-trump-congress-constitutional-crisis

John B. Judis
The Paradox of the American Democracy, Elites, Special Interests, and the Betrayal of Public Trust
Pantheon Books, New York, 2000

Steven Levitsky & Daniel Ziblatt
How Democracies Die
Broadway Books/Penguin Random House, New York, 2019

Vejas Gabriel Liulevicius
Turning Points in Modern History
The Teaching Company, Chantilly, 2013

Thomas E. Mann und Norman J. Ornstein
It's Even Worse Than It Looks
How the American Constitutional System Collided with the New Politics of Extremism
Basic Books/Perseus Books Group, New York, 2013

Sarah Pruitt, "When Did African Americans Actually Get the Right to Vote?" January 29, 2020, Accessed 2/23/2022, https://www.history.com/news/african-american-voting-right-15th-amendment

John Rawls
A Theory of Justice
Belknab Press, Harvard University Press (Cambridge MA), 1971

Thomas E. Ricks
FIRST Principles, What America's Founders learned from the Greek and the Romans and how that shaped our country
HarperCollinsPublisher, New York, NY, 2020

Roland Rich
Democracy in Crises
Lynne Rienner Publishers, Boulder, CO, 2017

Daniel N. Robinson
American Ideals: Founding a "Republic of Virtue"
The Teaching Company, Chantilly, VA, 2004

Clinton Rossiter
Parties and Politics in America
Cornell University Press, 1960

Mark A. Stoler
The Skeptic's Guide to American History
The Teaching Company, Chantilly, VA, 2012

Encyclopedia.com, [2022] "Political Parties In Constitutional Law", Accessed on 2/23/2022
https://www.encyclopedia.com/politics/encyclopedias-almanacs-transcripts-and-maps/political-parties-constitutional-law

History.com, [2021], "Constitution", October 27, 2009, Accessed on 2/23/2022
https://www.history.com/topics/united-states-constitution/constitution#:~:text=%22We%20the%20People%20of%20the,for%20the%20United%20States%20of

Goodreads.com [2022], "Election Quotes"
https://www.goodreads.com/quotes/tag/elections

What Would The Founding Fathers Tell Us Today?

What Would The Founding Fathers Tell Us Today?

Lightning Source UK Ltd.
Milton Keynes UK
UKHW022111190722
406102UK00009B/76